What I Learned in School

What I Learned in School

REFLECTIONS ON RACE, CHILD DEVELOPMENT, AND SCHOOL REFORM

James P. Comer

JOSSEY-BASS
A Wiley Imprint
www.josseybass.com

Published by Jossey-Bass A Wiley Imprint 989 Market Street, San Francisco, CA 94103-1741–
www.josseybass.com

Readers should be aware that Internet Web sites offered as citations and/or sources for further information may have changed or disappeared between the time this was written and
when it is read.

In the interest of readability, the editors have slightly adapted some of the selections for this
volume. For the complete text, please refer to the original source.

Limit of Liability/Disclaimer of Warranty: While the publisher and author have used their
best efforts in preparing this book, they make no representations or warranties with respect
to the accuracy or completeness of the contents of this book and specifically disclaim any
implied warranties of merchantability or fitness for a particular purpose. No warranty may
be created or extended by sales representatives or written sales materials. The advice and
strategies contained herein may not be suitable for your situation. You should consult with a
professional where appropriate. Neither the publisher nor author shall be liable for any loss
of profit or any other commercial damages, including but not limited to special, incidental,
consequential, or other damages.

Jossey-Bass books and products are available through most bookstores. To contact Jossey-
Bass directly call our Customer Care Department within the U.S. at 800-956-7739, outside the
U.S. at 317-572-3986, or fax 317-572-4002.

Jossey-Bass also publishes its books in a variety of electronic formats. Some content that
appears in print may not be available in electronic books.

Page 165 constitutes a continuation of the Copyright page.

Library of Congress Cataloging-in-Publication Data

Comer, James P.
    What I learned in school: reflections on race, child development, and school reform / by
James P. Comer.
        p.   cm.– (Outstanding ideas in education series)
    Includes index.
    ISBN 978-0-470-40771-4 (cloth)
        1. Comer, James P.   2. Educators—United States—Biography.   3. Education—United
States.   4. Education—United States—Philosophy.   5. Child development—United States.
6.   African American children—Education.   I. Title.
LB885.C5255W47 2009
370.92–dc22 [B]

                                                                                          2009018597

Printed in the United States of America
FIRST EDITION
HB Printing   10 9 8 7 6 5 4 3 2

Outstanding Ideas in Education

The Outstanding Ideas in Education series offers an introduction to some of the leading thinkers in the field of education. Each volume in the series provides a thought-provoking retrospective of their work—in their own words—through seminal articles and essays. In presenting these monumental ideas in a clear and comprehensive format, each volume is designed to stimulate discussion and further innovation in the field.

CONTENTS

INTRODUCTION

What I Learned in School

DURING THE SUMMER OF 2007, I met then Senator Barack Obama at a fundraiser for his presidential campaign. The last time we'd met, two years earlier, I'd spoken with him about our School Development Program. I was not sure he remembered me, but before I could introduce myself, he said with gusto, "Dr. Comer! Are you still trying to save the world?" At some point later, it occurred to me that his comment closely echoed something Lee Shulman, president emeritus of the Carnegie Foundation for the Advancement of Teaching, said in his address at the 2007 Grawemeyer Award presentation. In his speech, Dr. Shulman spoke about people whose work seemed to be driven by a "saving the world mentality." That I might have such a mentality was a bit bothersome because it was a bit too close to megalomania, but the more I thought about it, the more evidence I found that I might indeed have world-saving ambitions. And when I consider some of my early thinking and behavior, it might be that I had such ambitions even as a young child.

When I interviewed my mother for *Maggie's American Dream*, her oral history and my related autobiography, she recalled a revealing incident. After my elementary school principal, Miss McFeeley, retired, she and my mother met in the local grocery store several times, and each time, she would tell Mom about this one memory she had of me.

Ms. McFeeley remembered, so many years later, something I said once after she finished scolding my three best friends. I said to her, "They are not bad; they just want to be loved." I'm sure that I deeply repressed the interaction because my eight- or nine-year-old's memory of my principal was of a fierce, seven-foot-tall woman who banged her large ruler on the table and brought complete silence to a hall full of noisy elementary school students lined up at noon one rainy day. I feared her immensely. So making our little world better must have been incredibly important to me, because I was not naturally courageous.

Now, as I put my reflections together, I sense that it was my impulse and desire to make all human relationships better that drove my curiosity, learning, and scholarship over a lifetime. The school I learned from was more than the formal education institutions I attended and worked in. Growing up in America in the 1940s—I was six years old at the turn of the decade—as a black male from a family on the lowest rungs of the working-class ladder, with high mainstream aspirations and expectations, sensitized me to obstacles and opportunities. The best chance for someone from my background to be successful was to live and observe life with a raised level of consciousness about obstacles and problems and to consciously devise ways to overcome them. As such, I was engaged in participant observer research and intervention, a type of research in which the researcher comes to understand the contextual meaning of activities and behaviors by participating as a subject. And by chance, my observations were made during the most pivotal and perhaps instructive fifty to sixty years of American history.

The Intersection of Race, Schools, and My Research

Although I did not ask how I might fix the world, I did ask how I might be helpful to capable children who were not going to have an opportunity to be successful. Perhaps it was a recognition that the world was too big and complex to tackle but that education was a little piece of the world that the faith and hope of my parents had made extraordinarily important and evidential to me. In addition, the changing nature of the economy suggested that education was going to be important to all, more than ever before. These factors led me to position myself for work in schools. And as it turns out, schools are strategically located and education is the crucial ingredient needed to fix the world.

When comparing my approach to studying education with those of my colleagues at the time, I was perhaps less concerned with certain aspects of the research and intervention strategies than many of them. Instead, I focused more on whether the work answered real-world questions and could be used to solve real-world problems. This was so much the case that I agreed not to write about our initial work in schools unless participating parents agreed that our findings might be useful to similar students elsewhere. (In the late 1960s, activist low-income communities were challenging researchers about using their children as guinea pigs in order to advance their own careers.) An agreement like the one I made with the parents could have been career suicide in the publish-or-perish environment of academia, but it turned out to be a blessing and a source of great insight for me.

Our Yale Child Study Center team began our work in 1968 with a pilot study and intervention in two elementary schools in New Haven, Connecticut. Our charge was to understand why these schools were underperforming and to find ways to greatly improve them. While we observed and worked in the schools full time and helped devise interventions, I used the time I would have used to write about the work in schools to explore and write about racial issues—the elephant in the school and in the rancorous streets in cities across the country. The more I explored, the more I realized that race is a very real, omnipresent, deep, difficult, painful, complex problem. I also realized that the issue of race is more about power, security, and adequacy than about individual or institutional racial prejudice. The simple answers offered and labels given in the mid- to late 1960s certainly created targets of blame but could not provide effective pathways to conflict reduction or resolution.

During this time, I realized that many academic researchers were trying to understand and address racial issues and other complex problems with tools and methods that did not take into account crucial, critical, hugely powerful influences—such as human nature, history, culture, experience, and individual internal and external situations or conditions—all of which interact in complex ways. Our national struggle to overcome the ill effects of slavery; the effects of experiences of exclusion from participation in mainstream political, economic, educational, and social structures, with consequential impact on families and child growth; constructive adaptations that in many cases are characterized by resilience and hope and the opposite (hopelessness, apathy and withdrawal, and acting-out behavior)—all these and many more interactive forces, influenced by changing technology, economy, and culture, are potentially in play not just when black and white individuals and groups interact but when any two groups interact.

This realization led me to rely on a holistic approach that meant taking everything into account and then determining what was important in school—in teaching and learning. The kind of tangible, quantifiable variables or factors needed in experimental research designs cannot capture the complexities created by human feelings, attitudes, values, hopes, and dreams. And the findings from such research usually can't help educators create interventions that address such issues. I also found that the diagnosis-and-treatment approach of medicine was helpful, particularly its emphasis on understanding the disease or problem before applying the treatment. Our work in schools looked at how students learn and what they need in life and then at how all the people, structures, processes, and activities in a building interfered with or facilitated learning—diagnosis—and we then made adjustments as indicated—treatment.

In education, there was and still is an emphasis on curriculum, instruction, and performance assessment, with inadequate attention to understanding students' needs and learning challenges among the students and in the school environment.

A holistic approach in which we considered forces beyond the time and place of the school—and their interaction effects—helped us to understand troublesome conditions and behaviors among students, staff, and parents that led to low school performance. We then began to devise the "treatments." By helping staff to apply child and adolescent development principles to support student development—our understanding of what students need to live and learn well in school—we were able to create school climates and then cultures that greatly reduced the ill effects of human nature, history, culture, and difficult experiences that were at the root of racial and other conflicts in schools; often, we could create well-functioning, high-achieving schools.

I was struck by how quickly racial conflict among and between staff and parents decreased when structures and processes evolved that made critically important interactions and conditions possible for them: shared power, responsible participation, self-expression, and creativity. These in turn promoted mutual respect, trust, security, and collaboration. This environment and the improved student development and learning that followed strongly supported our notion that environment, development, and academic learning are interactively and inextricably linked.

The Way to Approach Student Development and Learning

I saw parallels between the transformation of the two low-performing schools in New Haven and the civil rights movement. The movement was pressing for more widely open and accessible political, economic, educational, and social systems—the essential elements of an effective modern democracy—envisioning a process very much parallel to the way that shared power and responsible participation helped to turn around our pilot project schools. It was my thought and hope that education could change broadly in this direction and that the education enterprise might help lead the nation in its effort to create a more effective democracy—might help to fix America. As it has turned out, the civil rights movement sparked other movements that have improved our political, economic, and social systems and created a better democracy. But instead of leading the way, our education system has lagged, failing to prepare enough people to keep our economy strong and in the lead in global economic competition or adequately prepare our young to effectively participate in, protect, and promote our vital democratic institutions, particularly in the community.

Evidence suggests that education has failed to adequately prepare students because scientific and technological advances have changed the way we live but schools and many families and communities have not adequately changed the way they prepare our young people to learn and live in this more complex age. Our experience in more than forty years of implementing the School Development Program (SDP) suggests that the underlying problem is that to be successful in school and in life in the twenty-first century, many students need a higher level of development and need to be intentionally prepared for adult life. Yet we find that many families, communities, and schools are not able to provide these. Our current educators were and our new workforce of educators continues to be prepared to pass on the traditional approaches to teaching, learning, and testing, including adult control of student behavior.

Over the last ten to fifteen years, national policy and programs have promoted a business management approach to improving our education system—establishing standards; instituting program changes and coaching in curriculum and teaching; testing student and teacher performance, and implementing sanctions when goals are not achieved. A strong indication that the management emphasis, innovative curriculum and instructional programs, and changes in the education delivery system are not working to the extent necessary is that more than 45 percent of all new teachers leave the profession within five years and far too many who survive are less than highly effective and highly gratified. And the student outcomes across the socioeconomic spectrum are less than what we need to survive and thrive as a nation.

We believe that the most efficient and effective way to meet the needs of our students in a deep and systemic way would be to prepare our education workforce to *integrate student development and academic learning* in all aspects of learning from school entry through student maturity (P-16), with a focus on promoting student personal responsibility in preparation for meeting life tasks. Without this kind of intentional qualitative change in what happens in interactions between students and school staff, all school improvement programs and service delivery arrangements such as charter schools and vouchers can provide only scattered sites of excellence at best and cannot be sustained. They do not address the underlying needs. At present, the workforce that is prepared to meet the needs of modern students is much too small.

Our nation has been at school reform for more than fifty years. The time for experiments and noncrucial innovations—"Let all flowers bloom"—as the major approach to improving student achievement should be over. In the same way that builders start with the foundation regardless of the style of the home, so too must we in education begin with addressing student developmental needs, the foundation for human learning. To create a world-class, nationwide system of education, we must first understand that our primary focus must be on the student interactions with teachers and administrators and prepare a workforce that can routinely create effective interactions. Changes in public policy and in the preparation of the education workforce as well as adequate support for effective practice will be needed to create and sustain a large enough pool of effective practitioners and resultant good practice everywhere.

This book provides a deeper exploration of the ideas I have outlined in this introduction. Seven chapters drawn from four of my nine books as well as the Grawemeyer Award introduction and lecture present my experiences and learning in the school of life and in formal schools. It is a pleasure and a privilege to have this opportunity to reflect on how my personal life, mission, and purpose have influenced my training and work and to share my reflections, not as an answer but as a persistent question: Why not prepare a workforce to support the development of the whole child?

Finally, and with much appreciation, I thank the many parents, students, and school and district staff members who helped us learn; the colleges and universities who worked with us; my colleagues at Yale who supported a somewhat different approach to research and scholarship; the Rockefeller Foundation and many others, particularly my colleague, Dr. Edward Joyner, who for almost two decades brought his education knowledge and skill to the task of preparing other people to use the SDP's conceptual framework to bring about change; other SDP colleagues; and many others.

The following words were offered by David Reynolds at the Grawemeyer Award ceremony at the American Educational Research Association's 2007 annual conference, held that year in Chicago. David Reynolds is professor of education at the University of Plymouth and professor emeritus at the University of Exeter, both in the United Kingdom. His contributions helped establish school effectiveness and improvement as a field, and he has published nineteen books and over two hundred papers and chapters. In 2007, he was one of three judges on the Grawemeyer International Committee, which awarded James Comer the prize that year for his book, *Leave No Child Behind: Preparing Today's Youth for Tomorrow's World*.

INTRODUCTORY REMARKS AT THE GRAWEMEYER AWARD CEREMONY

DAVID REYNOLDS

IT'S A VERY GREAT PLEASURE AND AN HONOR to say a few words about Professor Comer and the reasons why we chose this particular book [*Leave No Child Behind*]. In many ways, it's a book that exemplifies a tremendous contribution and a tremendous life of scholarship.

There are three judges on the international committee: Sam [Stringfield], Larry Cuban, and myself, representing all the non-American nations of the world. [*Laughter.*] It's two hundred and twenty-seven, I think, and, well, I try.

We should say that last year we were unanimous and this year we were unanimous, which isn't to say we didn't discuss and we didn't argue, but the decision was unanimous both years.

Basically, I think the importance of Professor Comer's work and his contribution is as follows . . . and we're really talking about the

xviii   INTRODUCTORY REMARKS

School Development Program, which he took from two schools, I think, in 1968 and built into, I think, four figures of schools currently. And his school improvement design, which is achieving huge effects in transforming children's life chances.

So what is the marvelous content of Professor Comer's work? Firstly, it's holistic in the sense that it deals with all the aspects of children's development. It isn't fixated on test scores, as many governments—indeed, some educational researchers—are.

It looks at children in the round. It looks at the affect. It looks at the emotional. It looks beyond simple academic outcome measures. In fact, it looks beyond outcome measures and actually wants to get into the study of things like school processes. So it's holistic, in a world in which many things aren't.

Secondly, the work is about pulling all levers that might affect the outcomes and processes within schools. It is remarkable to see the evolution of the School Development Program over time, because almost everything that we could take from the school effectiveness and school improvement communities, Professor Comer's been doing. There are parent programs. There are reading programs. There are management initiatives. There are interventions at the level of the community. Virtually every single body of knowledge which would lead to a lever, Professor Comer and the School Development Program pulls.

And I think the great thing about this use of multiple levers is you stand a chance of getting the interaction effects, which you don't get clearly if you're doing just one or two things. And I think . . . the success of the program [is that it does] an awful lot of things which individually may have quite small effects which, potentially, together have much larger effects, which actually marks out the quality of the program.

Thirdly, Professor Comer's work, whilst it's theoretically informed, is empirically based. Whilst being aware of the difficulties of measuring everything and sometimes the difficulties of clearly measuring what matters, the School Development Program has been built by studying which bits of it worked and, crucially—and here's the honesty—which bits of it didn't.

The context in which it worked, the context in which it didn't, the necessity of adding new bits in certain context[s] to make it work—it was built out of careful empirical study about what worked. It wasn't just produced by theory, even though it was theoretically informed.

If you look at most school improvement, I would say the great majority of school improvement, it is nothing like Professor Comer's work. It often basically doesn't evaluate what it does. Often, what it does seems to owe more to the needs of the individuals (to have better hearts or better souls or feel better about themselves) than actually to the need to improve the outcomes and processes of schooling.

Very often in school improvement, people just worship in different churches. They go out performing, well, some have called it random acts of human kindness, with no measure about whether they work or not, and go back happy.

Well, Professor Comer worships at a very different kind of church. It's a church called Truth. And I think that's marked out the quality of his work in that program.

Fourthly, I think Professor Comer shows the value of sticking at a patch and tilling the ground over and over and over again and not moving on when things are tough.

There are descriptions in this book, in *Leave No Child Behind*, about test scores which remain stubbornly rooted to the ground, about problems that the projects run into. And very often, people respond to that by going to do something else, a different kind of research project, or going to a different geographical area. [But] Professor Comer really for a long time was in one area and for a long, long time has been in this one field, perfecting a school improvement design which can truly help the world's children.

Lastly, I think the great thing, and it was brought back to me reading the book again just recently, the great thing about Professor Comer and his work is the intellectual and personal honesty within it.

I have never seen anybody write down the list of research grants he had, which were unfortunately discontinued by very stupid foundations, in the way that Professor Comer [lists them]. I mean, which of us has said, "Look, we ran into problems here because we had no money. We were scurrying around trying"—which of us has said, "We were scurrying around trying to find new sums of money to keep this going." That degree of intellectual honesty is very, very marked. And you compare that with the self-promotion of academics, the pitching, the simplifying, the hiding of things because they won't fit into a media sound bite or won't appeal to governments. [When] you read this book of total intellectual and personal honesty . . . it's really very, very striking.

I'll conclude on an English soccer story about probably the greatest soccer player of all time. Have you heard of him? Called Martin Peters. *[No response.]* That's interesting. That makes the point of the story better, I hope. It's an interesting thing that you haven't. . . . He played for the United Kingdom World Cup team in 1966, when we won it. He was probably the greatest soccer player ever.

The trouble with Martin Peters, and it's why you haven't heard of him like you've heard of Pelé. Pelé? *[Audience responds affirmatively.]* Yes; okay. *[Laughter.]* I was just being—of course, I was being cautiously empirical about this.

The reason why you haven't heard of him is that people said of him: that he was twenty years before his time. He was just too good. And what would happen is Martin Peters would be out on the pitch and he'd play a pass. He'd do a soccer pass, and he'd play the ball over there, and heck, there was no one there to receive the pass because the rest of the teammates just weren't thinking through that's where the ball's going to go. He was just ahead of the game. And I think Professor Comer is, in a sense, your American Peters.

It has taken time, I think, for people to, as it were, run onto the pass that Professor Comer's been making all those years about *holistic*, about a *full range* of children's needs being addressed, about *pulling all levers*, about the *careful empiricism*.

I think, basically, it has taken the dysfunctional society which we increasingly inhabit, the absence of mesh, the absence of community networks, the fragmented nature of modern society to make it clear that his approach, because of its emphasis on the social and the community as well as the academic, is one, maybe even the *only* one that can save your public education and public education around the world from the creeping privatization, from the differentiation into different settings with different cultures and ethos that one sees.

I think basically old Mr. Grawemeyer would be very pleased, as we all should be, for this recognition of the tremendous work and the lifetime's achievement—[for] education, the society, and the world in general—of James Comer. Thank you very much. *[Applause.]*

ADDRESS AT THE GRAWEMEYER AWARD CEREMONY

*American Educational Research Association
Presentation, Hyatt Regency, Chicago*

JAMES P. COMER, 2007 RECIPIENT OF THE GRAWEMEYER AWARD IN EDUCATION

THANK YOU VERY, VERY MUCH FOR THAT VERY GENEROUS INTRODUCTION. And thank you all for that very warm reception. And I thank you, Lee Shulman, for your kind comments and, really, the setup for the presentation I'd like to make today. Also, I'd like to thank Sam [Stringfield] and all of the people connected with the Grawemeyer Award for my selection and for this opportunity.

The Grawemeyer Award and this session have special meaning to me. And David [Reynolds] has now given it even more special significance. Many of the comments he made I have felt, but it would not have been appropriate for me to say. So I greatly appreciate his introductory comments.

Lee mentioned that my work at the intersection of psychiatry and education was like standing at the intersection of State and Madison here in Chicago. While many of my colleagues have encouraged me to do what I am doing, I was the only one doing it differently from traditional psychiatrists, so that the intersection often felt like a lonely place. This award has validated the approach in a way that is very nice—and very important.

Lee's comment about a desire to save the world also resonated with me. I often felt that I was trying to repair the world and thought it was kind of megalomaniac. But I really think that education—and getting it right—could go a long way toward saving the world, so . . . I was happy to hear my work put in that context. What I'd like to do today is to talk briefly and then have time for questions; to talk about my big idea in education, where it came from, what we did with it, where it is now, and what we are still trying to do. To do this, I would like to begin with a brief discussion of my childhood and how my experiences and those of my childhood friends led me away from a plan to become a general practitioner of medicine, into public health, psychiatry, child psychiatry, and, eventually, my work in schools.

While doing my internship in my hometown of East Chicago, Indiana—right around the lake—I began to notice that my three best friends were all going on a downhill course in life. One eventually died early from alcoholism; another spent a good part of his life in jail; and a third was in and out of mental institutions until he passed away. And other friends who had done well in school and who were bright were beginning to go on a downhill course. I asked myself, "What's going on? What is happening?"

Trying to understand, I began to read about race relations, the history of slavery, and the social sciences. But there was nothing in what I was reading that explained what was happening to my friends. And by the end of my internship, I was doing more reading outside of medicine than about medicine itself. I was being pulled by my curiosity—in time, my obsession. This led to a plan to do my military service time in the United States Public Health Service in

Washington, D.C., rather than go into practice immediately, with the thought that I could return and enter practice two years later if I did not find an alternate pathway.

While in the Public Health Service, I did volunteer work at a place called Hospitality House. It served children and families that had been kicked off the welfare rolls generally because a man was caught living in the house. These children were going to go on a downhill course. Much like my friends. I could see an impending crisis. The families could not provide them with what they needed to succeed in school. The nature of the economy was changing so that they would need a higher level of education to take care of them-selves and their future families. And the school was not prepared to help them.

An incident relative to an Easter egg hunt in school expressed the problem all too clearly. Hospitality House was a kind of boot-strap, private citizen volunteer agency, housing families that would have otherwise been homeless. I noticed a child crying in the cor-ner and asked him why. He told me that his teacher told him that if he did not bring a dime for the Easter egg hunt, he should not come himself. His mother was penniless. All of their belongings were piled on a box on the street corner in front of the house. I gave him a dime, and he went back to school. His mother was very grate-ful. But it was painful. The school was embarrassing and rejecting him and his family at a time when they were in need of help. While the school cannot help in every situation, it occurred to me that it could be more sensitive to the plight of the children it served.

Because of this and many other experiences, by the time I got to the University of Michigan School of Public Health in 1963, I was deeply interested in family and community issues and what could be done in these settings to prepare children for school—all chil-dren, not just the children of the well-educated, well-functioning, and good-income families. In a term paper I wrote during that year,

I argued that schools should work to build on the strengths that children and families bring and compensate for what some children did not receive prior to school.

I decided not to go back to general practice but instead went into psychiatry and eventually child psychiatry. Public Health had helped me learn about institutions and the interactions of people in them. I needed to learn more about people of all ages.

But where did this obsession—a need to know and need to intervene—come from? Why was it so important to me? It was my own background. I am from a low-income family. My mother was from rural Mississippi and had less than two years of formal education. My father was from rural Alabama and had a sixth-grade rural education. He worked as a steel mill laborer and my mother as a domestic. The two of them eventually helped the five of us go to college, where we were able to earn a total of thirteen college degrees.

My mother's life was particularly difficult. She was born to a sharecropper who was a very good man, but he was killed by lightning when she was six years of age. Because there were no support programs, a cruel stepfather came into their lives. He was abusive in every way and would not allow the children to go to school. They lived under very bad conditions.

When she was about eight years of age, she decided that the only road to a better way of life for her was through education. When she was sixteen, she ran away to a sister in East Chicago and tried to go to school. But the sister didn't support her efforts, and eventually, she had to leave and become a domestic worker. But when she did, she declared that "If I ever have children, I'm going to make certain that all of them get a good education!" And then she set out to very, very, very carefully find my father. *[Laughter.]* As it turns out, my father had been married once before and had a daughter, so she wasn't sure that he was the right one. She insisted that he provide her with a letter of recommendation from his ex-mother-in-law before she would go out with him. *[Laughter.]* But it worked out well.

Reflection on my story deepened the question about what happened to my friends. Our parents had the same kind of education and jobs, and we attended the same school—a predominantly white, working- to executive-class school. My friends were just as bright as anybody in my family and anybody in our school, and yet they all went on a downhill course. Eventually, I realized that the only difference between us was the quality of the developmental experience that we received at home. And it was that understanding that helped me begin to think about what could be done in school to make it possible for such otherwise able young people to be successful.

Because it was a major source of insight, I want to tell you a little bit about my developmental experience. Nurturance was a very big and important part of it. Every Sunday evening, my mother would read us the funny papers. Funny papers are not great literature and my mother could just barely read, but that is not what was important. What was important was that two of us would be down in front of her, leaning on her legs, and two of us would be on her lap. We would squeeze in as close as we could, and she would read us our favorite part over and over, until she had read the paper two or three times. It was the nurturance, the closeness, the warmth that made reading a positively charged experience. Also, my mother and father would take us to the Lake Michigan Park so that we could play and they could interact with us. There was malted milk, popcorn, and popsicles on our front porch on warm summer evenings. All of these were homemade; they were giving something of themselves to us and saving money.

With this kind of nurturance, children can believe in themselves and develop aspirations and hopes. So that when the doctor came to see me when I was about four years of age, when he left, I said,

"I'm going to be a doctor when I get to be a big man!" My parents responded to that by buying me a doctor's kit, playing with me, and reminding me that the candy pills were for the patients, not the doctor. *[Laughter.]* A lady from our neighborhood came by and saw them playing with me and said, "Why are you encouraging him to be a doctor? We are poor people; you know that he will never be a doctor." My mother said, "Say that one more time, and you will have to leave." So not only was promoting the aspiration important, but protecting from naysayers was equally important.

Also, young children must gain knowledge and skills about how to interact socially to be able to make it in the world. We learned many of them around our dinner table. Every day, we were expected to be there on time, talk about what went on in school, listen to each other, express ourselves, and so on. The discussions would often lead to after-dinner debates or arguments. We were competitive, energetic, and wanted to win. But there was a rule that no matter how badly you were losing the argument, you could not fight. And so I found myself coming home from school practicing my argument, thinking through how I would present it, how to express it, because you could argue, but you couldn't fight. I was gaining personal control and self-expression capacities mediated by my parents in a warm, supportive environment with rules and expectations for responsible conduct.

We were exposed to everything my parents believed to be educational—the museums, the Bud Billiken Parade [an African American festival in Chicago], shopping at the downtown Chicago department stores during the Christmas holiday season, and other events. When President Roosevelt came through our hometown, they bundled us up and took us down to see his entourage come over the bridge. On one occasion, my mother was working at the election poll when I came by. She invited me over and into the polling place, which was probably against the rules. I actually pulled the lever for her vote—which was against the rules. *[Laughter.]*

But the exposure to what the adults were doing—and getting involved with them—was exciting and motivating. They taught us all of the skills necessary to present ourselves well in all these situations, to enjoy, and to learn. These experiences at home were the platform for school success.

We even learned problem solving by observing our parents. I watched them on many occasions. They never raised their voices, but they thought carefully about the situation, marshaled their facts, and presented effective arguments. Years later, when an English literature teacher gave my two white colleagues an A and gave me a B—when we were one, two, and three points apart at the top of the class—and she gave a person thirty points behind me a B, I asked her for an explanation. We talked over a half an hour, with her insisting that a B was a good grade. Finally, she said, "Well, you know, I just don't think you are capable of making an A." End of argument. I knew what that perception meant. Those were the grades for the first ten weeks. I went back and worked very hard over the next ten weeks. and at the end of that semester, I was at the top by one point. She gave me the A I deserved. That's the way I've been taught to face such problems: Never let the way you respond to injustice justify your mistreatment. Force people who mistreat you to take a good look at themselves and their motives.

All that we did and learned at home was reinforced in our primary social network of friend and kin and organizations that were important to our family. In our case, this was the Zion Baptist Church. Also, the church gave me a strong sense of belonging in an institution that was larger than our family, and at the same time. all of the major ideas, values, and expectations were the same as those in school. But in the church, there was no sense that your right to be there was conditional.

All of the interactions that took place between us and our parents and family and then within our primary social network supported our overall development. The interactions promoted our physical development, including development of the brain, and enabled our parents and other meaningful people to mediate our social-interactive, psycho-emotional, moral-ethical, linguistic, and cognitive-intellectual development. Our experiences channeled our energy—aggressive and potentially harmful—into the constructive energy of learning, work, and play. We gained the competencies, confidence, and comfort needed to operate in settings beyond the home and the primary social network. It allowed me to think, "I can." In increasingly difficult environments and settings, I was able to believe that I could manage; thus, when we went off to school, we were prepared to make a positive attachment and bond to school people just as we had done at home. We could believe that we would be successful in school.

The power of that preparation was shown again when I came back to visit my mother in the hospital almost twenty years ago. My eighty-plus-year-old first-grade teacher was a volunteer. When she saw me, she threw her arms around me and said, "Oh, my little James!" I was fifty-five years old. *[Laughter.]* But you're always "my little James" to your first-grade teacher. Then she stepped back and said, "Oh, we just loved the Comer children." She continued, "You came to school with those bright eyes; you got along so well with other children; you were so bright. . . ." She went on and on. What was she describing? She was describing the outcome of the developmental experience we received at home.

My three friends who were probably just as intelligent had a very different experience in school. One example: Our fourth-grade teacher designed an activity to encourage us to use the library. We were expected to get a library card, take out and read books, and report on them in school. I read the most books and won the contest. My three friends had not taken out or read any books. My teacher responded angrily, "If you three little colored boys don't want to be like the rest of us, you should not come to our school!"

My teacher was not a die-hard racist. I walked to school hand in hand with her every morning. She had worked hard on an exercise that was important to our learning experience, and my friends just weren't cooperating. She was frustrated and disappointed. But if she had been taught to understand child behavior, she would have explored and learned that my friends were the grandchildren and great-grandchildren of sharecroppers, tenant farmers who were intimidated by mainstream institutions. If she had understood this, she would have taken them by the hand and helped them take out library cards and participate in the exercise. But she didn't. This created confusion for me. I knew that this teacher—and almost all of my teachers, all white—meant well and treated me and my siblings well. Why was there a problem between some of my teachers and some of my friends?

This question didn't emerge fully until I finished medical school and was doing my internship. As I struggled to understand why my friends were going on a downhill course, I recalled an incident which first suggested that this might eventually be the case. When I went off to college the first time, one of my three friends came by to say good-bye. As he left, we continued to talk through a screen door, me from inside the kitchen and him from the outside back porch. A little tear rolled down his cheek. It was a sad moment, but there was more than sadness there. It was like standing on the caboose of two trains backed up to each other, going in opposite directions. I was going on the train up to opportunity, and he was going on a train that was going to lead to a downhill course. It struck me as unfair and not necessary. That reflection and many others during my internship led me to volunteer service and the training that landed me in schools.

During my training in public health and prevention, and having fully realized that the difference in the outcome between me and my friends was the quality of my developmental experience, I raised the question of whether it was possible to approximate my experience in schools and thereby improve the outcome for students who did not receive adequate preparation at home. Leading social scientists of that period were saying that it could not be done.

Fortunately, the late Dr. Albert Solnit, then the director of the Yale University Child Study Center, did not accept those findings and invited me to direct a joint school improvement effort between the Child Study Center and the New Haven Public Schools. In 1968, our team—two social workers, two psychologists, and a special education teacher (and later one social worker, one psychologist, and a special education teacher)—went into two pilot schools in New Haven. There was very little guidance because the school improvement literature was small and not very helpful. We did not find literature that linked family and community functioning, child development, and school performance. Almost all the literature started from a deficit perspective. There was something wrong with the kids, their families, or the community. The substance and process of schooling was rarely, if ever questioned. But the way teaching and learning was understood and carried out was a major part of the problem.

A mechanical model undergirded the thinking about teaching and learning—the good brain, bad brain notion that some children had good brains and others didn't. You should expect different outcomes, given that situation. Development did not play much of a part in the understanding. The experimental research design was the preferred approach among education researchers, but it is quantitative and based largely on student performance outcomes and is not holistic. As such, it could not tell us very much about what was going on in schools. Although I was skeptical about using this research design, Dr. Solnit and I reviewed this approach with Dr. Bill Kessen, a highly regarded psychologist at Yale. We all agreed that it was not appropriate for what we were trying to do: to understand why schools failed to serve so many able students. Also, our numbers were not large enough to provide us with quantifiable data. I remember Bill Kessen saying, "Don't worry about it; do it! This work is too important to worry about whether we do it the preferred way or not." After we developed an effective model and involved enough schools, we did both qualitative and quantitative research.

In 1968, racial integration in schools was being pushed as a cure to education and social problems in the society. But I had seen my three friends and other African American students with good ability not do well in racially integrated schools with white teachers who wanted to be supportive. And there were African American students who did do well who were from low-income backgrounds like my own. It appeared to me that racial prejudice was a contributing factor, but not the critical underlying problem. I was beginning to believe that student underdevelopment and inadequate staff knowledge and skills to compensate . . . [were] the root cause of poor school performance. An early experience in our pilot school work supported my budding hypothesis that when students receive support for development, they are more likely to behave well and do well academically in school.

We had a youngster who was in rural North Carolina on a Friday in a warm, supportive network of friends and kin. Over the weekend, a visiting aunt brought him to New Haven and, on a Monday, dropped him off in our pilot school. Without preparation, he was taken directly to his new classroom. His teacher had just had three transfers in and out of her classroom the week before and, with a nod of frustration, unintentionally transmitted rejection to the new student. Alone and anxious, he kicked her in the leg and ran out. We social and behavioral science types thought that that was a pretty healthy response for an eight-year-old. But of course, his teacher didn't.

When our mental health team discussed the incident with the staff, we pointed out that the child became anxious as a result of the loss of his supportive community and being dumped in a strange place with strange people. The principal and teachers understood, and made in-class and in-building adjustments that made it possible for this child and many others to come and go and function well in school under more supportive circumstances.

As I finished discussing this incident with the teachers, I made what I thought would be a comical comment, understood by all. I mentioned that this was interesting in that here was a case of fight *and* flight rather than just fight *or* flight. But not a single teacher understood what I was talking about. They all looked at me as if I was speaking a foreign language. Fight or flight is a basic behavior concept that every beginning social and behavioral science student would know. And yet teachers on the front line working with children didn't know it, and many even now don't know it. This was absurd, unfair to the staff and the students.

This experience strongly supported my hypothesis. The students were underdeveloped, perhaps differently developed, and simply behaving as such children behave under challenging circumstances. The teachers were, through no fault of their own, underprepared and not able to respond in ways that would help the student[s] grow. The underdevelopment and the underpreparation led to difficult interactions in this and many other situations and to a downhill course for the students, teachers, and the schools.

Change was needed. But there was a problem. You can't simply mandate change. You can't explain child development and expect teachers and administrators to apply this knowledge appropriately. And it wouldn't help, as an outside expert evaluation team suggested, for us to do it ourselves. A reconceptualization of how children learn and behave and how to support it had to take place among the staff so that the change would be organic. We put in place a framework that allowed our social and behavioral science team to infuse the knowledge into the everyday work of the school staff and parents. This made it possible for them to change the culture of their school and support the development of the children in a way that would lead to improved academic learning and to the acquisition of the knowledge and skills that would prepare them to be successful in school and in life.

They eventually took a developmental perspective to all that went on in the school rather than thinking of the students as good or bad. They took a nonjudgmental, nonpunitive but mediating and guiding approach. This approach, applied to every aspect of schooling, helped to create a school culture that prevented problems and promoted development and learning. One example of an outcome: A nine-year-old who had been in three schools in the prior semester and each time had had to fight his way in, came to our pilot school. Somebody stepped on his foot during an exercise, and his dukes went up; he was ready to fight. Another child said, "Hey man, we don't do that in this school!" The would-be fighter looked around because he had not been in a school like that before. The expression on the face[s] of the other children reflected agreement: "We don't do that in this school." He dropped his dukes, and he didn't have to fight his way in. The children had become the carriers of the culture of the school that had been established by parents, school people, and the students working together. The resultant reduction in behavior problems allowed the school to focus on teaching and learning.

As the students grew along the developmental pathways—again, the physical, social-interactive, psycho-emotional, moral-ethical, linguistic, cognitive-intellectual, academic—the schools were transformed from places of conflict and poor academic performance to good development and high learning communities. Importantly, these improvements took place without a specific and required curriculum and instructional approach. This has been the case in all of our work.

The big idea finding, then, is that schools can approximate support for a developmental experience that will help students grow and learn even when they do not receive sufficient support prior to school, that it is possible to infuse knowledge and skills into schools in a way that enables school staff to gain the capacities needed to create a culture needed to help students perform well. This was an affirmative answer to the question I raised as a public health school student.

After a field test of several years in different parts of the country, we began to disseminate our child- and adolescent development-centered big idea and the framework or model we created in which to carry it, the School Development Program (SDP). When we began the large-scale dissemination phase, we created a training program in which we worked with several schools of education; Youth Guidance, a social service agency here in Chicago; and we continued to work directly with some school districts. (I see my good friend and colleague Vivian Loseth, now the director of the Youth Guidance program, in the audience. Thank you, Vivian. She brought our SDP to Chicago at a time that I was concerned that we would get lost in big cities. Youth Guidance was able to help a number of schools in Chicago make significant gains, as demonstrated by a study that used a random-assignment experimental design.)

Before Chicago, we disseminated the SDP in individual schools, then in clusters, and eventually we began to work districtwide. We repeatedly encountered significant resistance. We worked toward a districtwide approach to get support from top leadership in order to try to overcome a resistance to change that we noted from the beginning, even in our pilot schools. In our pilot schools, we overcame resistance by working with people who wanted to change, and when they were successful, others either changed or left. With clusters, where we had less direct contact and influence, we noted that about a third of the schools improved dramatically, about a third improved a bit, and about a third didn't improve at all. The outcomes reflected the degree of acceptance and resistance of local leadership and staff.

Several schools of education teams, working with our SDP team, worked with districts to create highly successful programs. And pre-service education students from their colleges and universities gained firsthand skills and knowledge about how to apply child and adolescent development principles in practice. We had hoped that the teachers and students from the colleges would influence and encourage their teacher and administrator colleagues to give more attention to the important role—even, centrality—of child development in education. There was polite discussion and, in some cases, related coursework changes, but no substantial change in the colleges or universities took place and many of the changes that were made were not sustained with turnover of university and district staff.

There was little we could do about this in working with the colleges and universities. But with districts, as mentioned, we reasoned that if we worked with the top leadership—superintendents, school boards, others—there would be sufficient positive sanction to overcome much of the resistance. Beginning in 1998, we began to work with five different school districts. All five districts made significant gains over a five-year period. Asheville, North Carolina, did particularly well, and they were the only district where a racial comparison was possible. Thus, I will discuss this work here. Please look at the first PowerPoint slide.

You can see that 1998 was the first year. By applying the principles of the School Development Program, they all but closed the racial gap in reading in five years. The same was true in mathematics. The lowest-achieving school initially, Hall Fletcher, had the highest percentage of African American students. Their third grade had 41 percent student proficiency in reading, 94 percent five years later; 43 percent in mathematics, 97 percent proficiency five years later. By fifth grade, they had 100 percent proficiency in reading and 100 percent proficiency in mathematics. Over the five-year period, the number of low-income students increased but the proficiency rate increased.

Why were these changes possible? Why is the SDP effective without a particular instructional program? In fact, it works with any adequate instructional program. To answer these questions, let's go to the next PowerPoint to review our conceptual framework.

Our observations suggest that students who are born into mainstream social networks have the best chance of experiencing support for development that will prepare them for school and for achieving life goals. They have the best chance of developing well along all the pathways that I mentioned previously.

Children from nonmainstream families are more likely to have difficulty when they enter school because they are more likely *not* to have developed in a way that would allow them to elicit a positive response from school people, as was the case with my childhood friends. They are more likely to struggle and/or not do well in school. Prior to the 1960s, such students might well have been successful as adults with no or little education. With the passing of the agricultural and industrial eras and the loss of farm, factory, and high-paying, low-skill jobs that did not require a high level of education, many more students who drop out or do not do well in school become heads of households but are under economic and social stress.

As a result, there are more families less able to give their children the experiences needed to prepare them for school success. These and other factors contributed to the breakdown of many families and communities. Because of these powerful societal structural changes, we have now seen three generations of downward mobility and marginalization among families that were poised in the 1940s to move into the social and economic mainstream. Many such children and families were served by our pilot schools. The difficult interaction between underdeveloped or differently developed students and school staffs not prepared to support development led to the low-performing schools we encountered.

Our School Development Program, or school transformation model, shows nine structures and processes to help the parents and staff to create a culture inside of the school that enables them to greatly improve the development and learning of students. This positive outcome takes place in spite of difficult conditions outside of the school.

The School Planning and Management Team (SPMT) is the engine and overseer of change. It is representative of parents, teachers, and administrators. It was primarily through this body that the principles of child and adolescent development were infused and applied to all that went on in the school. The SPMT carried out three operations: the creation of a comprehensive school plan that was both social and academic; staff development based on goals established by the SPMT; and assessment of development, teaching and learning, and modification based on the findings.

The Parent Team had representatives on the SPMT, and they contributed in ways that supported the overall school program, both social and academic. And the Student and Staff Support Team—social workers, psychologists, special education teachers, and other professional support staff—were represented on the SPMT, and they worked in a coordinated, cooperative, schoolwide preventive way wherever possible rather than in a fragmented, individual student problem-fixing way. Only when student needs were not being met by the improved school social climate did they work with individual students or small groups. They brought in community support resources when needed.

Because we can't expect people who don't know each other, like each other, or trust each other to work in cooperative ways, we developed three guidelines. The first was no-fault decision making. The focus was on solving problems rather than pointing the finger of blame. The second was consensus decision making based on the developmental needs of children. And the third was collaboration. These guidelines were used first by the School Planning and Management Team, and eventually, they permeated all the activities and interactions in the schools. The culture changed from one of control and punishment, with much resultant acting out by the students, to a commitment to mediate and support the development of students. This led to higher academic and social behavior expectations and the expectation that they would increasingly take responsibility for their own growth and development.

A school culture that does not facilitate support of student development, desirable behavior, and academic learning is more at the root of our nationwide school problems than anything else. Poor student performance sets in place a series of actions and reactions that begin in the classroom but reverberate and cascade in complex ways across all areas of the education enterprise— classrooms, schools, districts, workforce preparatory programs, state departments of education, and other practice leaders and policymakers at every level—ultimately creating and maintaining low-performing systems. Many schools using our SDP, working collaboratively toward goals they themselves establish[ed], in a rewarding environment, achieved accountability among the participants and schoolwide that was more powerful than external sanctions and had outcomes that were not expected, particularly for students from nonmainstream backgrounds.

Where are we now? The SDP model has been used in more than one thousand schools, and we have repeatedly demonstrated that where there is sufficient buy-in . . . [on] the approach among school staff and parents, schools serving low-income children can be greatly improved. In fact, a focus on development improves the performance of all students. We have been evaluated many times— twelve external evaluation studies, two using random-assignment study and comparison groups. Geoffrey Borman and his associates, in a meta-analysis of twenty-nine comprehensive school reform programs, showed that only three improved test scores. Ours, the SDP, was one of the three, and we did not focus on test scores, and we did not require a particular curriculum or instructional program. This suggests that changing the culture of the school in support of student development is as important and perhaps more important than the current heavy emphasis on improving curriculum, instruction and assessment, and/or strict accountability measures.

But throughout the education enterprise, there is still great resistance to a child and adolescent development focus. This is the case because the traditional beliefs, attitudes, values and the most common ways of thinking and working in education are deeply entrenched within the institutions of the enterprise and strongly held by people within or who pass through them—from teacher to parent to state legislator. The resultant inability to change is probably the major reason that more than 45 percent of all new teachers leave the profession by five years after they enter. The reasons they give for leaving are more tied to the absence of a child and adolescent development perspective than those commonly thought—low pay, class size, low status, etc.

The traditional model of teaching and learning works for too few. But even most school reformers have given little attention to the centrality of student development and its relationship to academic learning and preparation for later life. It is for this and other reasons that after more than fifty years of modern school reform, we do not have widely improved student performance, particularly the performance of students from nonmainstream backgrounds. Knowledge from neuroscience over the past twenty years suggests that student–parent and teacher interactions and/or support for development actually construct the brain, and supports the long-held but often dismissed concepts of developmental scientists and some educators about how learning takes place and the most useful approaches to teaching. But even this hard science is not being responsibly integrated into school staff preparation and practice and research.

As a result, we continue to go around in circles, rediscovering approaches used thirty and forty years ago, giving them new names, and holding them up as the next great hope. And in frustration, we blame the failure to improve education on particular groups and conditions—teachers, their unions, administrators, parents, television, and so on. And yes, the way our K–12 educational system is funded is a major problem, but not one that we can do a lot about in the short run. But . . . demonstrating . . . high-level social and academic learning among many students thought not likely to perform well, through staff and parent application of child and adolescent development principles, could move us toward a widely improved system of education.

How can this happen on a large enough scale to move entrenched practice? Because adult mediation of development is critical, parents, teachers, and administrators must be prepared in pre-service and early in-service to think and act as if it is critical, to understand that development and learning are inextricably linked and how to embed academic learning into everyday and school social and emotional development and academic activities. This will require preparatory institutions to work differently and will require practice leaders and policymakers to empower preparatory institutions to work differently. It is when parents and educators have the knowledge and skills needed to support development and learning that standards, testing, and other assessments become useful and fair, when accountability will become a useful tool of improvement and not just an attractive slogan.

Again, our SDP tried to work with departments of education, state universities, and school districts in ways that bring these important entities together to begin to prepare teachers and administrators to be able to apply child and adolescent development knowledge and skills in practice, but we lacked the economic and political power to do so. It is my impression that only a cooperative effort between state and national government, related preparatory programs, and local districts can make this happen.

Widespread school improvement must happen soon. We cannot keep up with domestic, global, economic, and social changes that are taking place in the country and in the world without a system of education that is based on the developmental needs of students. While too many of our schools are underperforming and too many of our students are falling behind, we are not yet beyond a point of no return. With knowledgeable leadership, our system of education can be turned around, can be among the best.

With that, I'll stop and respond to questions.

Thank you very much.

1

Washington Elementary School

When I joined the Yale faculty in 1968, I was reluctant to use my personal experiences as a source of insight, as a data base. But I needed to understand the different outcomes for me and my siblings as opposed to those for my friends, and with the encouragement of a few colleagues, I came to understand my experience as a unique window on complex and challenging problems. This perspective led in 1972 to the publication of *Maggie's American Dream: The Life and Times of a Black Family.* This short chapter is an illustration of the complex way in which race, class, family, and culture issues can play out in school to create challenges and opportunities, and how parents and other authority figures interact to protect and promote a child's effort and capacity to negotiate his or her environment and acquire a solid platform and springboard for lifelong performance.

MY FIFTH BIRTHDAY WAS THREE WEEKS AFTER THE START OF SCHOOL. Mom had to entertain her club at our house that day, so she arranged to have a party for me at school. I loved being the birthday boy.

The next day, one of my white classmates begged me to take a different route and walk by his house on the way home. His mother was hanging laundry on the back porch of their second-story apartment. He called up to her triumphantly, "Ma, this is the boy that had the party in school yesterday!"

The mother looked at me quizzically and said, "You didn't really have a birthday party, did you?" I indicated that I did. "Well!" she said. "It's the first time I ever heard of a nigger having any kind of a party but a drunken brawl." She turned and walked into the house. I was too young to fully understand. But I knew that she said something bad about me. I cried.

That incident was unusual. All four of us—me, Norman, Charles, Thelma—were occasionally invited to the birthday parties of our white classmates, and we were always treated well. I didn't tell mom what happened after my kindergarten party, but she was cautious anyway and always called to make certain that the parents knew that we were black and to determine whether we were welcome or not.

At one birthday party, the party boy's mother told us that we were all welcome and that she wanted us to all have a good time. I was the only black kid there, and she looked at me with a big smile and said, "And you too." The other kids appeared puzzled by the special recognition—I was one of the gang—but they dismissed the comment and kept going. I understood, felt a little uncomfortable, but also kept going. Being one of the gang was important to me, maybe no more than to any other kid, but maybe more. I still remember that when we exchanged valentine cards in the second grade I got seventeen—the second highest total in the class.

This was the same Washington Elementary School that my oldest sister Louise had gone to more than a decade before. It still served the highest-income group in our town, but now served a larger number of working-class white families. Because the black families lived at the fringe of the school district, there were only three other black students in kindergarten. The only black staff was the school janitor. But the school was a real part of the community, and I felt like a part of the school.

I used to go shopping with my mother, father, brothers, and sisters at the A&P Store in the neighborhood every Friday. We would see somebody from our school there almost every time—Miss McFeeley, the principal; the school clerk; one or two teachers. "How are you?" "Fine." "How are you?" And "How is Jim doing in school?" It was tough to do anything but behave properly and work hard when your parents were in contact with school people like that.

Mom never missed Parent Visitation Day. She was always well dressed and seemed to get along well with my teachers. Norman told me that he was glad Mom came because he noticed, as a little kid, that the kids whose parents came to school received more attention. Robert English, a black classmate of Norman's, said that he didn't want his mother in school because "she might embarrass me in front of these white folks."

There were occasional problems. Mom didn't sidestep them just to get along. Once I heard her on the telephone, talking calmly but forcefully to our principal.

"No, I don't teach my children to fight. I teach them not to fight."

(Pause.)

"I most certainly teach them to defend themselves—whatever way necessary. Even you admit that Norman didn't do anything to that boy. He was bigger, and he was sitting on Norman's head. I would expect him to bite him or do whatever else is necessary to get him off his head."

(Pause.)

"If there's a charge for the doctor bill, we'll pay it. But I don't expect my children to let anybody walk over them."

I was about nine at the time. And another incident from that period stands out in my memory. At that awkward age, there was nothing about me that resembled a swan, black or white. I wore thick glasses, had buck teeth—earning me, in 1943, the nickname "Hirohito." One day, the gym coach had us going through calisthenics. I didn't perform very well. That weekend my friend Madison

Turner was teasing me about having to duck-waddle as punishment. Mom overheard, connected the sore muscles I had with the punishment, and was ready to take on the coach on Monday morning. I was awkward, generally the last person chosen for gym class softball teams. Now I was going to be subjected to the ultimate embarrassment, my mother going to see the coach! But when Mom called on Monday morning, she discovered that the coach had had a heart attack over the weekend and died.

The rational side of me understood that it was a medical illness. But his death confirmed a small irrational side of me that said, "It's dangerous to take on Mom."

One year, Charles got an unsatisfactory warning note—the infamous pink letter. Mom had the four of us in the car driving down Columbus Drive, then still the major way to get to Chicago, when she chose to deal with Charles about his poor performance. He had a special way with Mom and could provoke her far beyond her tolerance level with me and Norman.

She said, "You can do better than that!"

He knew that there must be a mistake, but he said, "No, I can't."

"You can!"

"I can't."

"You can!"

"I can't."

Finally, Mom got so frustrated she stopped the car in the middle of the street and said, "You can!!!"

Mom was not the best driver in the world, nor was Dad, for that matter. I was always a bit nervous when we got in the car, although I always wanted to go. But this was more than that. We were stopped in the middle of Columbus Drive, the busiest street in town—right in front of the main fire station. Cars were whizzing by, and I could imagine that at any second, the fire engines would roar out of the station. I was terrified! I could have choked Charles. Tell her you can, and get us out of here, I thought to myself!

As it turned out, a mistake had been made. The teacher was new in the school and didn't know our family. There were only two black kids in the class. The unsatisfactory notice was intended for the other black student.

It appeared to me that good grades could save me from a lot of grief, at home and at school. Even my buddies from the neighborhood approved. The black kids walked toward our section of the school district together. When report cards came out, somebody would yell to somebody else, "The Comers got all A's again!" And the teasing would start—"That's why they got those big heads—headquarters. They have to store all them brains!"

Sometimes, though, academic excellence didn't help. I used to arrange to pass by Mrs. Weldon's house, my fourth-grade teacher who lived about two blocks from school, just about the time she was leaving. We would walk hand in hand to school. We got a gold star for every library book we read, and before long, I had the most gold stars of anybody in the class. Almost everybody else had read at least one book. But my three buddies, Rudy George, Nathan English, and Madison Turner, the three other black kids in our class, had read none. Mrs. Weldon was furious with them and lashed out in front of everybody: "If you three little colored boys can't be like the rest of us, you should not come to our school!" Her words stabbed me to the heart. This little colored boy never went by her house again.

The next year, I became even more race-conscious. To correct an overcrowding problem at Columbus School, black students were transferred to Washington School for the fourth and fifth grades. One of the few blacks at Washington and well accepted there, I was in the middle of the adjustment process. My sister, Louise, had been a teacher of the black kids from Columbus; thus, they were my friends also. And my father frequently talked of "our people"—black people. So where did I stand?

In one class, we selected a new set of officers on a weekly basis. After a while, it was clear to me that the whites were choosing whites—except for me—and the blacks were being closed out. Impulsively, I jumped to the floor and accused my white friends of doing so. When I sat down, it occurred to me that my white teacher might be upset. She sat in the back of the room and knitted while we carried out the mock government activities. I looked back to measure her reaction. She gave me a wink of approval. It reinforced what I had learned at home: you are supposed to fight for what is right. I became the middle man—diplomat of peaceful relations. After that, the white students began selecting some of the students from Columbus.

The real showdown came with Glen and Lincoln. Glen was a tough white kid, the brother of my friend David, whom I walked to school with almost every day. Glen had established himself as the schoolyard bully. Lincoln was the toughest kid from the Columbus School. They had had two previous fights that year, one won by Glen and one by Lincoln. And finally, the third was scheduled. The excitement swept the school. Everybody seemed to know about it except the principal and the teachers.

No direct racial incident caused the fight, but the black boys were on one side and the white boys on the other. Lincoln punished Glen badly, knocking him down three or four times. Suddenly, and unexpectedly, Glen dropped to one knee, his hands in a praying position, and begged Lincoln not to hit him again. The black kids cheered. The white kids turned away in embarrassment. I didn't like what I saw. Lincoln was my friend, but I didn't dislike Glen; he never bothered me. I didn't like the racial overtones.

Several of the black kids from Columbus were very smart, potentially as good academically as anybody in our class. During the summer between fifth and sixth grade, I went to a Sunday school convention and Bible study class along with five of the best students from Columbus, all girls. Everybody expected me to make the highest score because I often did so in the public school. But in the Bible school class, I had the lowest score. These girls didn't say anything at Washington School and weren't generally thought of as good students. In retrospect, I believed they scored well in the Sunday school convention class because it was a place where they were accepted and relaxed. They were intimidated in the public school.

By this point, it was crystal-clear to me that being a good student could save me from some of the indignities that my black friends experienced in school. The word was out. White equaled good and smart. Black equaled bad and dumb. If you were smart and black, you might salvage a little. For this reason, being the best, being perfect became very important—too important. Too many black students work under this pressure, even today.

For example, in my science class in sixth grade, I had twenty-four of the twenty-five questions on the test correct and I knew it. But I also knew the answer to the twenty-fifth; I just couldn't recall it. Finally, when the teacher wasn't looking, I looked in the book and got the answer. He caught me. He walked over, took my paper, tore it up, and gave me a zero. I stood up and my legs buckled, my throat went dry. It was the most embarrassing moment of my young life. I needed 100; I wanted to be first; I had to show that I wasn't dumb.

2

Me, Walter, and America

Beyond Black and White was published in 1972, four years after we initiated our work in the two pilot schools in New Haven. Walter (not his real name) was a real person from an early training experience, but in this chapter, he is also a surrogate for the many young people I had met before—classmates and friends—and the many I have met since in schools, prisons, and other places—potentially able people whose foundational experiences in families and communities did not prepare them to run a successful life race. Our focus during those first four years was on trying to understand what that foundational experience should be like and how schools and school people might work with families and community institutions to supplement and strengthen the foundation of students like Walter. America is changing, which I argued in *Beyond Black and White* must happen, but even now, despite much hand wringing and sloganeering about academic achievement gaps, our schools are not adequately addressing "foundation building" or preparing students for life.

IN 1968, WALTER STONER WALKED INTO THE CLINIC WHERE I was finishing my child psychiatry training and asked for help. He was assigned to a white female colleague, who, after the first interview, decided that he needed a black male therapist. Walter's chances of being treated by a black male therapist were negligible. At that time, there were approximately six black male child psychiatrists in the country. (Today, there are only about a dozen.)

I had a full patient load and didn't want to hear about another case. But my colleague was determined. She described a seventeen-year-old black youth who had terrorized several students and struck his male teacher. She felt that he was terrified by the ordeal of passing from adolescence into adulthood and could be served best by a therapist who could also be a model. As she explained her patient, a voice said to me, "That's exactly what you need, a ghetto tough to take up all the free time you don't have." But I was moved by her concern for Walter. It was clear that he did need help, although I thought from the beginning that he probably did not need a psychiatrist, that he was victimized by circumstances and conditions.

I came to our first interview expecting a mean, sullen, angry, tough guy. A very pleasant, round-faced, smiling youngster extended his hand and said, "Good morning, sir. I'm Walter Stoner." Walter was short and stocky, and alert to the point of being threatening. I could feel him reading me. But we took to each other immediately. He had a winning innocence and determination.

At seventeen, Walter was two years behind in school, although he had an IQ of 108 and his true intelligence was estimated by a psychologist to be at least ten points better than his score reflected. Despite his intelligence, he had been having difficulty in school from the beginning. He got into arguments and fights daily. He was the class clown, was good at turning the students against the teacher, and was popular with many of his classmates for this skill. He did some of the things that they were tempted to do but wouldn't. Of his own conduct, he would say, "I don't want to make nobody—the teacher or nobody—mad, but I just can't help it. I guess I'm just a born clown." As he spoke, he didn't look funny or happy. The tone sounded more like doom.

Occasionally, the intelligent, warm, and appealing side of Walter showed through. This aspect of his personality had attracted many helpers. He had tutors, and he voluntarily participated in special programs designed to help "underprivileged children." He had heard all the media propaganda urging youngsters to "Stay in school, or you won't get a good job!" In spite of the personal help and the propaganda, Walter was not making it in school, and he knew it. Because of societal and family pressure, he couldn't just quit. He had to set up a situation that would get him thrown out. When that didn't work, he finally did quit, with the rationale, "They were gonna get me anyway."

Leaving school caused another conflict. He had been completely taken in by the American Dream/Horatio Alger ideal and was convinced that any American who worked hard enough would eventually be rich. Besides, he strongly adhered to the essential American manhood values. Referring to a man living off the income of a woman in his neighborhood, he said, "A man ain't s'pozed to depend on no lady. Lady s'pozed to depend on him! That's why I'm gonna be a football player and make a lot of money." He weighed less than 150 pounds, and his grades were too low to permit him to try out for the school team. When I asked about his actual chances, he brushed me off with "Look at Jimmy Brown, he made it!" He had a remarkable capacity for ignoring all the steps that would have to be taken to get from where he was to where he wanted to go. Walter harbored a magical notion that his hope would be realized without any change in his circumstances.

Magical thinking is an adaptive mechanism called forth when realistic opportunities for control of one's environment and destiny are few. Young children, slaves, prisoners of war, and nonscientific, nontechnological societies engage in a great deal of it. Even in a technological society, when a reasonable control by the individual of his own life seems unattainable, there is a rise in magical thinking. This phenomenon probably accounts for the increasing interest in astrology in American society.

Though only seventeen, Walter was the father of a nine-month-old son by his fourteen-year-old girlfriend. Determined not to be like his own father, he wanted to spend time every day playing with his youngster. On the other hand, he found it difficult to "be the man" while his mother was supporting him and the baby and while his girlfriend still lived with her mother. After he quit school, he held three different jobs in two months and talked longingly of going back to school. Had he gone back, he probably would not have remained, although he wanted to "be somebody."

Walter viewed himself as defective, unwanted, and vulnerable to attack by a host of more powerful, exploiting people, male and female. He lived among people who, overwhelmed by life's problems, cheated one another, lied, deceived, and occasionally violently attacked one another. Walter desperately wanted a different kind of life, but as he indicated, directly and indirectly, he felt that he was doomed to a similar fate. Most of the adults he had known well—parents, teachers, shopkeepers, policemen—had deserted, disappointed, or exploited him. Even the overindulgence and overprotectiveness of his mother and his grandmother were forms of exploitation, a way of gratifying their own needs. Overindulgence does not promote adequate personal control or a sense of security in any child. The attention and concern Walter got did permit him to develop some strengths, such as concern for others, sensitiveness, and determination. He sought, on the one hand, to be "the little man"—to protect himself and to control his mother, teachers, and friends. On the other hand, he wanted to be dependent, cared for, and secure.

He knew fear, but he had to deny it in order to feel like a man. Acknowledging his fear would have disorganized and paralyzed him. He constantly avoided the truth of his situation—leaving school, changing jobs—to avoid self-shattering personal confrontations. His dominant, yet least apparent response was profound rage so all-consuming it frightened him. He laughed uneasily about the conscious murder wishes he had once expressed toward his father. "Now I know better," he said. He handled his anger by playing a good-natured role in reality and fantasy: the helper of abused people, even the would-be philanthropist: "If I ever get rich, I'm gonna help all the poor children in Washington." He wanted to be loved, respected, and well known. During one session, he told me hesitantly that he had to become famous "even if I have to kill somebody." Only the week before, another psychiatrist suggested that Walter was the kind of youngster who, without a change in fortune, could lose his defenses and become a killer. Even if the outcome is less serious than that, it is likely to be unfortunate.

Walter initially had the basic biological endowment necessary to develop into a well-educated, productive citizen, and he still had the desire. But his gradually accumulated deficiencies in personal and educational skills, the rising performance demands from society, and racism past and present reduced his chances of becoming "the man."

His father deserted the family a few days before Walter was born. He had a rural North Carolina sixth-grade education and was ill prepared to provide for his large family. Three or four times after Walter's birth, he attempted to come back to the family, but it never worked out. Each time, there were constant arguments, primarily about his income, which was inadequate. Nevertheless, the father had to believe in his own manhood and deny his feelings of inadequacy. To do so, he drank heavily and became sexually promiscuous. This behavior, in turn, caused more family arguments.

Walter's mother was born in Washington, D.C. Her parents were from rural Virginia and were undereducated and unprepared for urban Washington life. They were hardworking but underemployed—a domestic worker and a government messenger. Mrs. Stoner had attended one of Washington's "custodial" schools—racially segregated, overcrowded, and badly neglected. She dropped out in the ninth grade. Within a year, her first child was born; within six years, Walter, her fourth and youngest child, was born. After the third child, the relatively satisfactory marriage had begun to disintegrate. Walter's most critical developmental years coincided with the most tumultuous events associated with the breakup of the marriage.

In a series of interviews, Mrs. Stoner described the conditions that led to Walter's difficulties:

> I stayed in the hospital four or five days after Walter went home. I was just so upset and nervous; it was the fourth baby, and my husband was gone. I didn't know how I was going to take care of them. When I got home, I was in bed for three or four months before I could begin to take care of Walter. By then, he hardly knew me. He was spoiled good. He was an ornery little boy and just as irritable as he could be. Cried all the time. He had a lot of colic too. His grandma spoiled him. She'd sit up all night holding him . . . . I used to cry a lot back then and worry about my husband. He was tied to his mamma. One while there, it looked like he was gonna come home and stay. But he couldn't get away from his mamma. She had all four of them boys, Walter's uncles, you know, tied to her apron strings. He wouldn't send me a dime. I know he didn't make much till he started hackin' [driving a cab], but looked like he would have taken care of his son. But he didn't.

Mrs. Stoner described Walter's early development:

> Soon as Walter was able to walk around, he was into somethin' all of the time. He'd tear up everything he got his hands on. Sometimes he'd get on my nerves so bad I know I didn't do right by him. I'd just get so mad I'd beat him too much. Mamma would scold me, and that would make it worse. He was a smart little rascal, and he knew just how to get us arguing, to get his own way. Funny thing about him: bad as he was, he was still scary. He'd walk 'round right under my dress tail, mine or mamma's, sucking

his thumb or carrying his bottle or teddy bear, till he was three, four years. I think he was still doing it when he went to school.

When Walter was four years old, his father came home and stayed with the family about a year. When he was sober, Mr. Stoner was very gentle and gave Walter much attention. However, during his drunken spells, he was threatening and violent toward his wife and children. Naturally, Walter was frightened during those periods and would run to his mother or grandmother for protection. By the time Mr. Stoner left the family, his drinking had gotten heavier and more continuous. When he left, the family went on public welfare. Mrs. Stoner reported that the first welfare worker assigned to her case was very understanding, but the second one kept confronting her with the suspicion that Mr. Stoner was still coming to the house and that Mrs. Stoner drove him away just to get on public welfare. Thus, aside from being overwhelmed by very serious personal problems, she was accused of wrongdoing by society's helping agent. This is not the way it's "s'pozed" to be.

The first year of life, like the first act of a complicated play, is the most important. The stars of the first act are the mother and the child. The plot involves the former helping the latter move from a helpless bundle to a one-year-old child, with rudiments of all the tools—relationship capacities, body control, speech, the ability and desire to explore, inquire, think, understand, and learn—necessary to take on the world. The mother must have certain skills and must receive specific kinds of support. In the optimum situation, the mother herself is mature and enjoys a reasonable degree of security—psychological, social, and economic. The mother's security is critical because the most important thing she can give her child in the first year is a sense of trust and confidence. Depending on her own level of confidence, development, and security, she either succeeds or fails to impart this sense to her child.

The father's primary function is to provide the mother with the economic and emotional security that makes it possible for her to give the child the nurturing he needs. To do this, he obviously needs a reasonably well-paying job that also offers some degree of job security. He cannot attempt even to look for such a job if he has not had adequate developmental experiences.

During the second and third years of life, the growing child has a number of important tasks to accomplish. He must come to appreciate himself as an individual and strive for self-expression and pleasure, but at the same time, he must learn to appreciate the needs and feelings of others. However, there is a pull to remain dependent, cared for, without restraint, unrealistic in thought and action. Against this is a developmental push toward independence, achievement, and recognition. Numerous tasks—self-care, sharing a toy, talking in turn—become projects around which children assert their independence by taking a positive initiative or by being negative and uncooperative, but they come to some agreement with their parents (to gain their approval and recognition) and thereby experience achievement and security. At the same time, they learn the rules of the world they live in. These many parent-child interactions help the child learn the realities of his environment, to reason, and to understand cause-and-effect relationships. For example, the toddler learns that if he persists in demanding a glass of water at 2 A.M., he eventually incurs the wrath of important loved ones, the major source of his sense of well-being and security. He learns to drink at other times.

Parents and adult caretakers, through firm but flexible and reasonable external control, help the child move toward greater inner control and self-expression without snuffing out initiative and curiosity. If the job is adequately handled, children enter the next phase with a fairly firm grip on reality, a positive self-concept, and a moderate degree of self-control, with less need for control by their parents or by society.

The period of life from three to six years of age is a time of intense relationship with the parent or caretaker. It is the time when a child begins to become like the parents, particularly the one of the same sex. Parents, teachers, or other important adults mold the child—usually without conscious awareness—toward the standards, values, and ideals of their own culture. Some children celebrate Chanukah and others Christmas Mass with little understanding of the meaning, but all are impressed and sensitized by the effect these events have on important family members. They will first imitate the others and then, usually, accept the event as meaningful for themselves. Through give-and-take with important adults and other children, impulsive behavior, raw hostility, and unrestrained self-gratification are brought under a greater degree of internal personal control.

During the period from six to twelve, children begin to develop the capacity for sustained work. Consequently, it is the time when most societies get involved in the planned and systematic instruction of their children. Even in nonindustrialized societies, it is at approximately this time that the parents begin seriously to train their children for adult tasks. Identification with dependable adults who can stay with a job and complete it is important if children are to develop such adult skills.

Long before entering school, many youngsters from stable families (which may contain either one parent or two) have been developing styles and skills necessary to acquiring a sense of industry and the desire to work. Simply being in a household where people are regularly getting up, organizing to be on time, and preparing for work transmits the notion that work and constancy are important and rewarding. Many youngsters at their play type or teach like mommy or carry a stethoscope or a wrench like daddy, practicing to become workers. Various aspects of middle-income living, such as goal setting, time orientation, and expectation of stability, give a direction and discipline to living that develop goal-directed and problem-solving behavior.

The capacity for sustained work in our society is, for better or for worse, also developed through mastering the basic academic skills and maneuvering through the social system of a public school. The child who can maneuver with relative success wins praise, develops a sense of adequacy and a need to be involved in productive activities. Failure in school may do just the opposite. Erik Erikson wrote: "Many a child's development is disrupted when family life has failed to prepare him for school life" (Erikson, 1963). As the child begins to move beyond the confines of the family and neighborhood and into the larger society, the things his family life have taught him are put to the test.

Obviously, Walter's experience did not prepare him for the test. Though he got inadequate overall care, he did receive a great deal of strict moral training, particularly from his grandmother. Walter's grandmother often scolded him and threatened him with the devil or hell because of his bad behavior: his tantrums, impatience, aggressiveness, and so forth. Walter described his grandmother's approach angrily: "I love her and all that, but sometimes she's hard to take. She'll say, 'Speak up if you disagree with me,' and if you do speak up, she'll say, 'You ain't got no respect for your poor old grandma.'" Respect for elders was important in Walter's home. Walter, Mrs. Stoner, and his grandmother went to a sin-conscious Baptist church every Sunday, but Walter quit at twelve or thirteen "'cause some of my men [friends] laughed at me." His grandmother cried for weeks afterward. In large part, the church and the values of the church talked about at home—work hard, be good, respect your elders, and meet your responsibilities—formed the basis of Walter's demanding value system.

In spite of his charge from home to achieve and be good, and his desire to do so, he could not do well in school. He was unable to sit still and work; his memory was short. Mrs. Stoner recalled, "He'd go from one thing to another; couldn't concentrate on nothing." In the early grades, he was often punished and forced to stand in the corner or in the hall. By the third grade, he began to take lunch money, clothing, and other things that belonged to his classmates. At this point, he underwent psychiatric treatment for about a year. His school performance was slightly better, but he was never able to overcome the stigma of being the "bad boy." When he was in the sixth grade, he and several other disruptive boys formed a little gang. Walter said proudly of this period, "Everybody in school knew our gang. We didn't hurt nobody . . . 'cept sometimes, but you got to look out for yourself in this world. Ain't nobody gonna look out for you. That's why I feel sorry for Benny [a friend who was not a good fighter] 'cause everybody mess over him."

Mrs. Stoner complained that the school was always requesting conferences with her about Walter. Because she worked as a housekeeper in the suburban community of Chevy Chase, she was tired from work and travel at the end of the day; having to go to talk about Walter was wearing and annoying. She said, "I couldn't do anything with him no way . . . 'Course I know it wasn't all his fault. Things at home weren't always the best."

One of Walter's most torturous periods was when he was ten. His mother and father were again having severe marital difficulties. Walter distinctly recalled what it was like:

I was so glad he came home, but before it was over with, I was glad he left. I tried. I gave him my bedroom, and I gave him my key and everything. Looked like he was glad to be home and looked like he liked us, but it just didn't work out. . . . He was sick! But back then, I used to think he was just mean, but he was sick. He used to go down the street and tell people, "This is my son." I liked that. But then you never could depend on him. He was always making promises he never kept. After he left again, we used to see him on the street and he'd say, "I'll be by the house next week, Tuesday." But he'd never come. We might not see him again for a month, two months. When he was with us, he was happy and looked like he liked us, but you just couldn't depend on him!

As he talked about his father, the anger in his voice was unmistakable.

As a result of Walter's chaotic childhood, he passed into adolescence with massive academic and social deficiencies. He read poorly, he could not spell, and he received more reward for teasing his classmates and teachers than for doing his schoolwork. Occasionally, he liked a teacher and would apply himself, but that would never last. He liked his tutor and saw him sporadically for two and a half years, but he did not make much progress. Special projects and books about Africa and Afro-Americans held only initial appeal for him; the only things that did interest him were action-packed comic books and football. However, Walter enjoyed school more than he realized. After he quit, he complained, "I miss the place bad!" The relationships he had with teachers and classmates, though fraught with conflict, were more fulfilling than his unsuccessful work experiences.

Mrs. Stoner said that during his adolescence, Walter was not dependable, that he was always looking for fun. She pointed out that sometimes he was in good humor and polite and at other times he was sulking and angry. During our sessions, Walter talked of the aspirations he had for himself as an adult. But he was unequipped and not able to concentrate long enough to make even minimal dreams come true. Mrs. Stoner noted:

He was always hanging out with the boys. I'd ask him why didn't he stay at home. He'd say, "There ain't nobody here to stay home with." I couldn't keep up with him. 'Course I couldn't blame him; he didn't have no daddy to take him places or nothing. He had a "big brother" once who was very good, but he left town. Another Big Brother was just like his daddy, always making promises but he'd never keep them. Walter started hanging out in the streets so much I warned him about getting into trouble, 'specially about bringing a baby home he couldn't take care of. But he was such a big man, he finally brought the baby home.

When she spoke of the baby, her voice and manner reflected anger. Mrs. Stoner declared that she loved the baby, but worked hard and had no time to take care of it. She complained that the baby's fourteen-year-old mother was immature and irresponsible and treated the baby like a doll. "Both of them's like two children rather than parents. Sometimes I say to the baby, 'Poor child, you ain't got no mamma and papa. You got a brother and sister.'" She felt that Walter tried hard at times to be a father but at other times forgot about the baby. "It doesn't look right to see him running down the street chasing four or five boys like somebody ten or twelve years old when he's got a baby upstairs to take care of."

Walter's background of failure and disappointment in school pushed him toward success on the street. The street—full of people trying to meet their relationship and achievement needs—beckoned to him. On the street, he fought well, bought a car, and made a baby. But his efforts to achieve brought him man-sized responsibilities before he had the social and emotional tools to meet them.

Adolescence, in the scientific and technological age, is a time for further development of academic, vocational, and social skills. It is a time for trying on, not taking on adult roles. It is a time when adolescents say to parents, "Go away and leave me alone until I find out who I am . . . but don't go too far." They will even ask a couple of questions to make sure the parents are still there. It is, in short, the time to establish an organizing, stabilizing, direction-giving personal identity. It is a time of ambivalence: adulthood, freedom, and uncertainty; childhood, dependency, and security. The anxiety adolescence engenders was greater for Walter because his desperate urge to be "a man" was thwarted as long as his mother had to take care of him and his baby.

While I was working with Walter, I often thought about how similar and yet how dissimilar we were. We resembled one another in appearance and in basic disposition; we were reasonably close in intelligence and aspirations. Our parents (except his mother) were undereducated rural folk, and we were from low-income families. But my developmental experience was the way it was supposed to be—except for the racial incidents. I did not know that we were poor. My parents were not part of the problem, but my dependable support. A promise was always kept. A chocolate bar was divided evenly to make sure that nobody was cheated.

Before I went to Hospitality House, I was still convinced that hard work brought success, that it was largely a matter of just deciding to work hard. I still believe it is important to perform to the best of one's ability. But getting to know Walter—and thereby getting to know more about myself—made it abundantly clear that good performance depends on more than individual effort. I was a product of a relatively good family, community, and educational experience, plus a little luck. From Walter, I got a partial answer to the important question "Who am I?" I am, in large part, more than me. I am what my family and society enabled me to be. He also helped me realize that there are too many people who are not making it because society prevents them from doing so.

Walter had been denied what a child needs to develop basic trust, regularity, security, and a sense of his own worth and value. As a result, he did not develop the ability to relate well to others and to accomplish his goals. Failure at work and play made it even harder for him to feel good about himself. He responded to failure and disapproval by aggressive teasing, fighting, and frustration. This, in turn, made his life even more difficult. Obviously, one can be rich or poor and be disadvantaged in the same way.

Although Walter worked hard in therapy, it was difficult to help him. His life was full of shattering social conditions and crises and limited in alternatives. His girlfriend was hit in the head with an electric iron by her mother. He quit his unrewarding job and had trouble getting another. Finally, he found a new job, but his car broke down and he had no way to get to work. It went on and on. His dreams of job success, returning to school, and eventually playing professional football collapsed under the pressure of heartless reality. He denied that his girlfriend's second baby was his (though it most likely was), so he escaped to the comfort of the United States Air Force.

Walter was not "sick" in the sense that he could not function. He might be classified as having an impulse control disorder or ego deficits. Even a paranoid flavor was present. His situation was what child development and behavior experts call "minimal psychopathology" (Senn and Solnit, 1968), but the label is not very useful. Walter had many more strengths than weaknesses. In fact, he was basically quite healthy: he had healthy desires, he had not completely given up, and he was a nice person. His primary difficulty stemmed from distorted, uneven, and maladaptive psychological, social, and intellectual development as a result of social and family conditions. One outcome was a lack of academic and vocational skill, and a poorly established work pattern. At the same time, his experience created in him all the hopes, aspirations, beliefs, and dreams of other Americans. Beneath all his defenses, he was perceptive, and bright enough to know that he was in trouble.

Walter is like too many other American youngsters, black and white. In fact, he was luckier than many. He was spared more serious psychological problems and intellectual impairment because of the care provided by his mother and grandmother. Many youngsters are even less fortunate because they have suffered even more complete neglect.

In a 1961 study of almost 400,000 children served by public agencies, one of every three was receiving attention because of neglect, abuse, or exploitation by parents or others responsible for their care. Approximately 50 per cent of these children were in foster care. About 100,000 had had two or more foster care placements (Welfare Administration, 1963, pp. 1–13). Many—no one knows how many—are shuttled between relatives and friends and never come to the attention of public or private agencies. Many move from place to place with their parents, often under disorganizing circumstances which in no way resemble those entailed in job promotion moves for middle-income people. Look in the record files of any poor urban school, and you will find children who have been in four or five schools by the time they have reached the second grade. In some schools, there is a 100 percent turnover of students in a single year. There is also evidence that the low-income family has a higher level of conflict than higher-income groups, a situation that often interferes with the development of relationship skills.

Children born to very young or immature mothers frequently have a difficult childhood. There is growing evidence that the quality of early mothering among the socially overwhelmed leads to inadequate intellectual stimulation and that the effects may sometimes be irreversible. The lack can also lead to patterns of behavior that will be disruptive throughout life.

One of the most troubled youngsters I have ever worked with was a seven-year-old Afro-American girl who had been shuttled around during the first three years of her life. Her mother was a prostitute in New York City, and her father was a narcotics addict. The unstable situation continued until she was adopted and received adequate care at three years of age. But it was already too late to overcome the damage that had been done. She was of average or better intelligence, but extremely difficult to live with. She manipulated adults, pitting them against each other in pursuit of her own personal pleasure. She was provocative, testing, and damned annoying, yet she was appealing and highly desirous of adult interest, concern, and care. Before I was able to establish a satisfactory relationship with her, she drenched me with water, rubbed clay on my clothes, threatened to throw paint on me, and ran out of the therapy room repeatedly. Elaborate efforts were made to keep her in public schools, but she was just too impulsive and destructive to make it. Her adoptive parents, though quite good, could not manage her. Psychiatric treatment on an outpatient basis was not enough. She needed to be placed in a residential treatment center, but adequate facilities were not available. At seven years of age, she gave every indication that, short of a miracle, she would not perform adequately as an adult.

There are people who point to the independence and aggressiveness of such children as evidence that they are not as seriously damaged as some claim. This is wishful thinking.

Children who do not enjoy the opportunity to establish good relationships between the ages of three and six may never develop the internal controls, the sense of right and wrong or of responsibility necessary to modulate and channel the expression of aggression and sexuality. These drives, unchanneled into depth relationships, curiosity, and intellectual pursuits, are manifested in excessive anger and hostility and appear to go into what could be called survival energy: doing whatever must be done to survive in a frightening world without the care and protection of a reliable adult. This may be bullying, bluffing, manipulating, exploiting, provoking others, and so on. Such behavior may not produce a negative feedback in the home, neighborhood, or subculture where it is common and even needed for survival—"You got to look out for yourself in this world. Ain't nobody gonna look out for you." But it is troublesome in school, in work, in love, and even in play. These are the children the teachers and the whole outside world call "bad." This was Walter Stoner.

The outcome for many such youngsters is tragic—especially if they are black. For many whites, such antisocial characteristics lead to minor crime. Because whites have more access to legal aid, they often receive minor or suspended sentences or they may be referred to psychiatric facilities. Such histories are much less a barrier to good future employment for whites than for blacks. I recall a white executive who left a psychiatric ward with suspended criminal charges and got a $30,000-a-year job. Some whites thrive in illegal rackets from which most blacks are closed out except for the "fall guy" role—the one who goes to jail during a crime crackdown. Indeed, some white youngsters with undesirable characteristics—those of a bully, a manipulator, an exploiter—eventually do well in politics and business, where such traits are all too often an asset.

For the black and the poor—without money for good lawyers, with poor education and training, and with extremely limited job opportunities after a minor offense—a jail sentence is much more likely than a psychiatric referral or a rehabilitation program. Jails across the country are filled with black youngsters who need residential treatment services, guidance, and direction rather than the higher education in bitterness, alienation, and crime that they acquire in prison. Black men are on death row for rape in this "civilized" age. Though rape is a serious crime, the death sentence is an excessive, cruel, and inhumane punishment. Few whites incur it.

But the extreme cases distort some issues, hide others, and even cast doubt on whether anything can be done. Children and families like the Stoners—extreme examples—are not the rule. It is my impression that most poor children, black and white, have an early developmental experience that could prepare them for the world of today. Even the Walter Stoners of America could make it in spite of the home conditions. Most do not need therapists; they need good schools. Many of our schools are not good; most of those serving the black and the poor are not good. But we are too quick in pointing the finger of blame.

Too many educators blame the children and their parents for the schools' failures. Too many parents and youngsters blame the teachers. Too many critics, who are not in the midst of the problem, cry for the children and assassinate the characters of the educators. What is wrong with the school is what is wrong with the family is what is wrong with the society. We are a society that has failed to gear itself to enable people to meet their basic needs. The failing public school system is only a by-product of this larger failure.

With the traditional American flair for ignoring behavioral complexities, the failure of our schools has been reduced to racism, classism, and lack of concern. Some researchers have even demonstrated with facts and figures that when teachers care, problem children can learn. On the other side, a group of scientists have facts and figures that prove that there is just something inherently wrong with poor, black children and their families. Would that life were so simple; it would be so sweet. But it is not. Teachers who do not care are the end products of a long process that is as destructive of them as of the children.

In the first place, intellectual and academic achievement is only one part of the school mission and only one part of what the student will need for adult living. The school also has an important role in promoting socialization and psychological development. Tests and measurements of academic achievement should not be the only indicators of the child's school success. Second, and more important, public education cannot be reduced merely to a classroom, a pupil, and a teacher. Education is a complex process that reaches beyond the classroom and into the chambers where social policy is formulated and financed. Unfortunately, it is not the social policy of today alone that impinges on today's education, but the social policy of yesterday and the day before that. To say if a child is not doing well that it's because the teacher is middle-class, racist, or does not care grossly oversimplifies a very complex problem. Teachers and schools have also been accused of programming children, dulling their senses, turning them off, destroying their sense of worth, and a number of other high crimes. I have known many young teachers and have not met one yet who entered a classroom determined to limit or destroy the development of any student. It is poor teaching conditions and techniques and our present system of teacher preparation that cause many teachers to do harm unwittingly.

The training of teachers is simply not on a par with the training of other professionals. Too many teachers are inadequately prepared for the classroom job. Most have been in college for three to three and a half years before they ever enter a classroom in a teacher's role as part of their formal training. This is unlike England, where teachers are in the classroom during every year of training. (Some of our student teachers discover at a late date that they do not like children or teaching, but having little alternative, they may choose to stay with their profession.) After a few weeks of student teaching, Americans can become certified and sent out as teachers to influence the intellectual, social, and psychological development of children. Young teachers from stable and middle-income homes are not likely to be able to cope with the sort of child who, not because she is bad, but as a reflection of her socialization, says to her dolly, "Shut up, you black bitch!"

Few teachers have had courses in individual, group, and classroom psychodynamics. They have learned educational theories and methods, but the application of these in real-life settings is often delayed until the baptism by fire on their first jobs. Theories are fine, but application is what it is all about. Some teachers regard impulsive children moving destructively around a classroom as curious scholars in search of knowledge. It is an easy mistake to make if you have never had an opportunity to study impulsivity in children. Opportunities for ongoing, supervised observation and analysis of successful teachers dealing with such problems are rare. Closed-circuit television and other technology are freely supplied for space and medical exploration, but too expensive for those charged with the responsibility of developing the next generation.

Unlike most occupational roles in business and industry, the teacher's is not simple and clear-cut. Children indicate their problems and request help in subtle ways. Walter Stoner was bright, had a difficult life experience, and desperately wanted help. In pursuit of this, he sought a relationship with one teacher in the only way he knew—a provocative, testing, teasing manner. He disturbed and disrupted the class in spite of himself: "I don't want to make nobody—the teacher or nobody—mad, but I just can't help it." The teacher, poorly prepared to understand and manage such children, perceived a personal attack and fought back. After one of Walter's provocations, the teacher read to the class a letter that Mrs. Stoner had sent him and laughed at the misspelled words. He warned Walter that he was going to be just like his mother if he didn't settle down and work. Needless to say, that approach only elicited more disruptive behavior. Yet disruptive, testing behavior is often a sign of health in children who have been abused and neglected. The task of the teacher or any caretaker is to help the child learn better ways to deal with his problems. Some teachers are intuitive and sensitive and can handle the most difficult situations. Most teachers, given adequate training, could handle them.

Teacher preparation also suffers from "advocacy training." The latest and most successful method being used, say, in Norway that catches the eye of the visiting professor from the United States can become *the* answer to the problems in Harlem, without being given critical evaluation. Some people with the answers for Harlem have never been in any community like it. In fact, many college professors preparing their students to teach in public schools have never worked a day in public schools themselves. When a professor with a pet method is popular and powerful and publishes prolifically, his method often catches on, whether or not it is applicable to a given child or community.

Too few teachers are trained to ask, "But will it work with some, all, or any of my students? Will it work in this community? Is it what the parents want for their children? Is it what the children need to learn how to handle their present and future environment? Will it facilitate their growth and development, or does it fail to meet them where they are?" A commitment to a given approach makes for personal security, but if the approach is the wrong one for a given child at a specific time, using it is a disservice. The children who suffer most from the inadequacies of teacher preparation are those who have had bad home experiences and come to school with developmental lags, and these include a disproportionate number of black children. But the inadequacy of teacher preparation is again only part of the problem.

Across the country, as blacks moved into communities and whites moved out, school systems were allowed to deteriorate. Even good administrations found themselves understaffed and forced to do some shabby planning. Alan Campbell, an educator, has pointed out that as economic activity became decentralized, business and industry began moving from the core city to surrounding areas, weakening the tax base of the city. This is a process that has accelerated rapidly over the past twenty-five years. For the thirty-seven largest population areas in the United States, the average education expenditure per capita in 1968 of the central cities was $82 versus $113 in the suburbs. The expenditure per student was $449 in the cities and $573 in the suburbs (Campbell, 1969).

Blacks are people who have had only two noncontiguous decades, 1920–1930 and 1940–1950, of even minimal opportunity on the job market in their 100 years of "freedom" and their more than 350 years in America. The consequences of this for family and community stability are well known. To prepare youngsters from a deprived community to cope as adults, the schools in the central cities should have been maintained at the economic and community support levels that existed before the whites moved out. In fact, an even higher level of support was indicated. Both compensation and reparation have been and still are indicated.

But even well-financed schools and school systems are very complex social entities. People with different professional backgrounds must work together as a team—teacher, paraprofessional, social worker, psychologist, psychiatrist, nurse, and administrator. In low-income areas, people of different income levels, races, religions, and political persuasions are working together, and the potential for conflict under these circumstances is high. The admixture of people and factors can be chaos or a symphony, depending on the management or orchestration the system receives.

Most of us who boast of caring more about people than about objects or money would like to ignore the fact that the school system is a business—with a human product. In fact, it is now big business, and it needs good management. It must be able to attract good personnel and serve their needs in ways that permit them, in turn, to serve the needs of the consumers—the students and families. School systems, because of politics and finances, must sit and wait, then accept whatever crosses their thresholds, while the personnel officer of a chewing gum company can traverse the nation in search of talent, and wine, dine, and woo the prospects into his business on a comparatively limitless expense account. A good business has the support staff necessary to keep its service staff operating at maximum efficiency. Few schools are able to do the same. A good business knows its market demands several years in advance and tools up to meet them. Most schools do not have the manpower or equipment necessary to mobilize for the year just ahead. New schools often start out overcrowded and chaotic because systems analysis and adequate planning are not available.

It has been traditional for school administrators to pick a teacher who has been successful in the classroom for ten or twenty years and make him or her an administrator. Often the choice is political and has nothing to do with ability. Although some so selected become excellent administrators, few of them are well prepared. Many fail. To strengthen school administrations, states are now requiring that administrators take a handful of courses, but these are likely to be theoretical and inapplicable to real-life conditions. Such is the training of the people who run America's most important business—the school.

Even if their preparation and training were adequate, many principals would still spend their time taking splinters out of fingers, holding the hands of youngsters who have been poked on the playground, unlocking doors (which should not be locked) when the janitor cannot be found—largely because most schools cannot afford to hire anyone else to do these things. The important management tasks—personnel recruitment, teacher support and development, curriculum planning, and so on—must often take a back seat to the day-to-day pinch-hitting for unbudgeted and unavailable staff.

The school administrator is also strapped by peculiar professional mores. Business generally does not tolerate incompetence, destructive attitudes, or carelessness. But we professionals are special people. We protect each other in spite of failures and shortcomings that hurt the consumer. The most that many administrators can do about incompetent personnel is to promote them or move them out of the way without firing or demoting them. Until recently, schools traditionally transferred their incompetents into school districts where the parents were least likely to complain. This was usually a low-income, migrant, and/or black school district.

It was assignment to Siberia for the teacher but a fate even worse—death at an early age—for the students.

Too few teachers in the neglected and troubled areas are able to do a creditable teaching job. Others make some kind of adjustment, not because they want to compromise their principles but because they want to survive. To fail is a threat to the teacher's sense of personal and professional adequacy, and like all human beings, he defends himself. For many, the obvious excuse is the child or his family; after all, everybody knows about culturally deprived or disadvantaged, hard-core children. What can one expect of the blacks, the poor, the lower class? "They don't care; they smell; they drink Cokes for breakfast; their parents are drunks." To survive, some run the classroom inflexibly. Others are too permissive, lower their expectations, and let the children do whatever they want to do. Many are overwhelmed and leave. Some are driven out, battered and torn.

This constant heavy turnover of teachers only increases the instability of the system. To look at a school and point with righteous indignation to teacher shortcomings alone is unjust. But such a school is the place where Walter Stoner and other children with bad home experiences get their second and maybe last chance. The Walter Stoners of America, without intent or malice, make it difficult for their classmates to get an education. When the school failed Walter, it was sabotaging more than one child's schooling. Like Walter, thousands of young people, a disproportionate number of them black, seek but do not find their chance in school.

It is into these deteriorating school systems that learned social scientists step—like clean, uniformed football substitutes onto a muddy field—with pencils, pads, and test papers, to measure achievement levels. They compare the scores with those achieved by children with two to five generations of good schools, good jobs, and family stability behind them. They determine that the poor children (often black) cannot learn as well as the children from more privileged homes (often white) (Bodmer and Cavalli-Sforza, 1970; Jensen, 1969). They pretend that achievement scores have nothing to do with the relative amounts of money put into black education and white education over the years and over the generations and even today. They ignore the fact that the under-educated students of the 1940s are the parents of the youngsters in school today.

It is unjust and cruel to focus on the child and his family alone and ignore the many other variables that affect achievement and learning. Social scientists only confuse the issue when they close their eyes to underfinanced, unstable school systems and under-trained, undersupported staffs while they focus only on the achievement of the child.

Child-, teacher-, and family-oriented research studies have contributed to a tendency to ignore a fourth party to the crime—those who appropriate funds, establish priorities, and develop school policy. This group is probably as responsible for the crisis in education as the other three, if not more so. Only the naïve believe that the school board alone is to blame. Business, industry, and government at the local, regional, and national levels are all involved. These institutions should be held as accountable for the plight of Walter Stoner as is the teacher who could not help him, the father who deserted him, and the school systems that undereducated his parents.

In addition, such studies produce simplistic solutions such as recommending that teachers care more, busing black children to predominantly white schools, and the establishment of a variety of compensatory education and enrichment programs. Even if such treatment of symptoms were practical and possible, it ignores the fact that the underlying disease is rooted in the social injustices and inequities of the past and present—including the traditional denial by our society of money for black education and the instability it still forces upon so many black families. Until these conditions are corrected, youngsters like Walter Stoner will present themselves to the school and society in rapidly increasing numbers and in a condition that our teachers and helping workers cannot deal with.

Of course, it is still true that failure in school is not always a life sentence to poverty, underdevelopment, and unhappiness. Some people find well-paying jobs and self-satisfaction without much education. For some, a special talent—singing, athletics, sales ability—will pay off. But school failure in this complex age generally spells trouble and low-level adjustment at best.

Predictions for life and living in the year 2000—less than thirty years away—stagger the imagination (The Staff of the *Wall Street Journal*, 1966). Population growth demands that technology move full speed ahead, or people throughout the entire world, including the technologically advanced nations of today, will be underfed, diseased, and in conflicts that could lead to world destruction. By the year 2000, the planet Earth will hold more than six billion people. It is estimated that there will be only six inches of coastline for every American by that year. Barley bread, fish, and the divine spirit will not feed this multitude! From one-half to two-thirds of the world's population live on the brink of starvation at this very moment. It will take skillful use of science and technology to feed, clothe, and house the generations to come.

Our society permits and exacerbates conditions that handicap children like Walter Stoner and his family, and then turns them over to the social worker, the psychiatrist, and other helping professionals and says, "Fix them." Too often, society has not provided enough people or facilities to do the fixing. I have seen many desperate parents, children, and school personnel looking for places where "salvageable children" can find help. I have often made phone calls and searched for days, only to disappoint the supplicants in the end. More important, we refuse to consider the possibility that the rehabilitation may be more than the helping professional can handle. The major disorder lies beyond Walter and his parents and teachers. Walter and others more severely disadvantaged are the primary victims of an inadequate social policy which cultivates racism and results in national priorities that put men on the moon before enabling other men to care for their families.

This may sound like an attempt at psychiatric justification for our societal ills. I grant that people are afraid to go out at night, that women are raped and men are mugged. Yet, the fact is that the marauders are also victims. (Walter possibly ended his failure cycle and probably his criminal potential by joining the military, but many others with experiences like his take antisocial directions.)

Many who commit antisocial acts are not simply "bad people." Numerous professionals who have worked in homes for delinquent children and in jails report that most inmates do not really want to be tough. Their behavior, for the most part, is the end product of a destructive developmental period. For example, I worked with one youngster from a troubled family background who would steal things from a nearby dormitory nearly every weekend. He knew that a youth home would offer more security than his own. He would be disappointed and angry when the judge repeatedly only shook a finger in his face and warned him not to appear in juvenile court again. Another youth pleaded to be sent to a residential treatment center because he had not been able to bring his destructive impulses and emotions under control in relationships with parents and adults. He was afraid he was going to hurt someone.

The neglected, abused, and exploited in one generation are often the exploiters and abusers of the next generation. One neglected and abused child in one generation may account for four in the next and sixteen in the third. It is this problem rather than too few police, too few streetlights, lenient court officials, and urbanization which is at the root of our soaring crime rate. It is, in large part, this that accounts for the fact that New York City has had more homicides in recent years than England, Scotland, Wales, Ireland, Northern Ireland, Switzerland, Spain, Sweden, the Netherlands, Norway, Denmark, and Luxembourg combined. (The overall population of these nations is approximately sixteen times that of New York City.)

There are thousands of damaged human beings who have not and never will come to the attention of public or private authorities and will therefore lead lives of personal misery—psychological and social. They will exploit and abuse friend, foe, and relative alike in search of a sense of personal adequacy in a world where they cannot earn enough to provide for themselves and their families. My patient in the emergency room, disfigured for life over a bottle of wine, was one of the victims. Walter's girlfriend, hit in the head with an electric iron, was another. All these people were denied the kind of childhood that might have permitted them to relate to others in a more humane way. Instead, they live now with day-to-day abuse, frustration, and anger which they displace on one another—killing, knifing, and beating.

But wait. Many people who live under terrible conditions can cope admirably. Most black people have made it. "You made it," I am often told. ("Making it," by my definition, means being free to relate to others in a humane way and being able to cope with the demands of any society.)

Yes, many people make it over every obstacle their fellow human beings put in their pathway. But too many who could make it with ease do not. People should not have to overcome colossal obstacles to enjoy a decent way of life. And on the way to success in this society, there is too much destructiveness among the seekers—pushing and shoving and cheating to get ahead and stay ahead. As a result, we have a conflict-ridden, exclusionary society rather than a cooperative, open society.

A situation I observed in one public school illustrates the point. In a midwestern kindergarten, a first-year teacher who was permissive had a classroom of total chaos. The most aggressive children destroyed property, harassed others, victimized the innocent and weak, and attacked the teacher. With a different teacher in the second year, kindergarten children from the same neighborhood and background performed quite differently. When property was damaged, it was accidental. Extreme aggression was rare and brought under rapid control—by the children more than by the teacher. A handicapped and vulnerable child in the class, who would have been a victim the year before, was helped to perform by others who took pride in that effort. It was no miracle. The teacher was well organized, attuned to the needs of the students, protective of the rights of each child. She set necessary limits and just expectations, established tasks consistent with classroom goals, and promoted individual effort and interpersonal cooperation. These are the requirements for peace, order, and achievement in any social system—be it the household, the classroom, the city, or the nation. The powerful people beyond the home and classroom—the policymakers—must serve the same function as the teacher or parent to accomplish the same ends. This has not been the case in America.

But it is too easy simply to criticize Uncle Sam. In spite of its shortcomings, the United States has a record of concern for people that puts it high among the nations of the world. (True, it has had a blind spot for black people.) It is doing better. It can afford to do much better. Its size, its heterogeneity, its frontier, its mentality and peculiar history have created a confounding complexity of issues that have delayed its confronting the fact that human needs must be met if a society founded on the principles of justice and equality is to survive.

A close look at the black experience reveals that black problems are simply the most extreme examples of American problems, that blacks have been only the most victimized by a generally inappropriate social policy. It reveals that, while black and white conflict is very real and painful, the root problem is *beyond black and white*. The black experience can teach us all much about how America must change if it is to reach and survive the year 2000.

References

Bodmer, W. F., and Cavalli-Sforza, L. L. "Intelligence and Race." *Scientific American*, 1970, 223(4), 19–29.

Campbell, A. K. "Inequities of School Finance." *Saturday Review*, January 11, 1969, 44.

Erikson, E. *Childhood and Society*, 2nd ed. New York: Norton, 1963.

Jensen, A. R. "How Much Can We Boost IQ and Scholastic Achievement?" *Harvard Educational Review*, Winter 1969, 39(1), 1–123.

Senn, M.J.E., and Solnit, A. J. *Problems in Child Behavior and Development*. Philadelphia: Lea and Febiger, 1968.

The Staff of *The Wall Street Journal*. *Here Comes Tomorrow! Living and Working in the Year 2000*. Princeton, N.J.: Dow Jones Books, 1966.

Welfare Administration, Children's Bureau. *Children's Problems and Services in Child Welfare Programs*. Washington, D.C: Welfare Administration, Children's Bureau, 1963.

3

Three Networks and a Baby

The subtitle of my 1997 book *Waiting for a Miracle* is *Why Schools Can't Solve Our Problems—And How We Can*. At that time, after almost thirty years of work, we had gained a deep understanding of the ways in which community and societal conditions affect families, schools, and student learning and behavior, but school improvement efforts were being tied ever more tightly to teachers, administrators, and students individually, as well as to accountability based on test scores. This book addresses the way conditions, policies, and practices beyond the school—economic, cultural, political, and other factors—affect teaching and learning and must be changed to account for student developmental needs if education is to be widely and significantly improved. This chapter provides a theoretical, empirical, and holistic framework for understanding how children and youths develop and learn, how major forces affect the process, and how the process could be modified or changed to improve education outcomes.

AT THE CORE OF OUR CULTURE STANDS THE BELIEF THAT A LIFE outcome is determined by the individual alone. The fact that this belief is so widely held speaks to the power of the pioneer ethos. But it is a myth. When you need two keys to open a bank box and you have only one, you don't get in. The individual is one key. The opportunity structure that the society provides is the second. Developing the individual and making opportunity available is the turning of the keys that determines the life outcomes of individuals and, thereby, the quality of life in the society.

Every child is born into three networks that influence his or her life. Imagine these networks as three concentric circles, with the child at the center of the innermost circle encompassed by another circle, which in turn lies inside a third circle. What goes on within these circles promotes or limits the development and the ultimate sense of power and security of the child at the center.

The innermost circle, the primary network, comprises the family, the extended family, their friends, and the institutions selected by them and accepting of them, such as their places of worship or fraternal organizations.

The middle circle, the secondary network, embraces services and opportunities such as the workplace, health activities, recreation, and schools. (We may consider work a human service: one's job is more than labor, since it provides personal organization and purpose.)

The last circle, the tertiary network, is the policymaking circle that includes local, regional, and national legislators and business, social, and religious leaders.

In the primary or family network, it is the heads of households (or heads of the extended family or, on occasion, of the church or club) who take the lead in interacting with secondary and tertiary networks to secure what they need to help their children to develop the capacities that *they* need—the capacities for making decisions and taking action—and the related sense of competence and confidence. These capacities grow with each success, and they are diminished or even lost with persistent difficulties. The process of growth, strongest throughout childhood, in fact continues over a lifetime, ideally producing an individual capable of acting independently, yet open to helping others and to accepting help from others.

All of the networks are affected by culture—that set of beliefs and attitudes and regular ways of behaving, on both the economic front and the aesthetic, that a group creates in its effort to thrive, to solve problems, and to find meaning and direction in life. Beliefs and attitudes that are pervasive may help or interfere with the functioning of the first network, the family. Cultural continuity and adaptive change from one generation to the next are both needed for a group and a society to have a good chance to function well.

We must consider how culture impinges on families and individuals—particularly as they confront the major family responsibility, the raising of their children.

The Baby and the First Network

Babies are born totally dependent, and yet by eighteen years of age, they need to be able to carry out all adult tasks and responsibilities. They need to continue to learn, work, live in families, rear children if they choose, and become responsible citizens. They are born with only biological and behavioral potentials (including a capacity for relationship) and aggressive and survival energies. The aggressive or survival energy can be destructive unless it is channeled and brought under the child's personal control. The relationship capacity makes it possible for caretakers to protect children from themselves and others—to limit their destructive potentials. The child's positive biological and behavioral potentials must be developed by all of the adults and institutions in the three networks of influence into which babies are born.

As parents of newborns hold and talk to them, a warm feeling begins to develop between the parent and the child. The parents take care of the child's food, clothing, safety, and comfort needs. The physical and language connection, emotional warmth, and comfort reduce the trauma of birth. Such care begins to produce what will eventually become a deep-seated inner sense of security and well-being in the child. "I am" begins here.

Children are programmed to seek attention and to please the caretaker. It is a beneficial survival arrangement but means that children are vulnerable when caretakers are not functioning well. As caretakers tend to the needs of their children, an emotional bond develops—particularly to mothers but now, more and more, to fathers as well. When the bond is adequately developed, its power enables parents to help the children grow.

Being a baby is like wandering in the north woods without a map, survival skills, or tools. In the beginning, the baby relies completely on the parents. For this reason, the very small child will not let the source of comfort out of sight and becomes one with the caretaker until growing confidence and competence permit a very slow movement toward independence. Meanwhile, the child experiences both gratitude for the support and resentment that the support is necessary.

The child's sense of self begins with the simplest of accomplishments. When a child first crawls, walks, and talks, attentive parents carry on as if the little one has made an earthshaking breakthrough. Children crave this, and they want to explore more and do everything their developing bodies will permit them to do— for their own pleasure and for the approval it brings them from the primary adults. They are excited about the world around them, and they probe and explore it relentlessly. As they explore, they jabber to themselves, pull on electric cords, touch hot stoves, run, and burst into laughter without apparent reason.

A knowledgeable parent knows when to encourage them and when to limit them in a way that does not turn off the interest but does keep them from harm. This enables children to learn the rules of the social interaction games—to learn to meet their own needs without compromising the rights and needs of others. Parents who see the significance of the jabbering will jabber back and add words. Those who ignore it or consider it strange and tell the child to stop will delay and limit the child's language formation and thinking.

Reading is critically important as a platform for future learning. Parents who recognize this begin to read to their children at an early age; some even do this before their child's birth (which is not totally wacky, for at least it puts the parent in the right frame of mind). Often, when a father reads to a little girl at the end of a busy day, it is the only time she gets him all to herself. She may curl up in his lap, sometimes in the fetal position with thumb in mouth. The reading experience has a positive emotional charge. My siblings and I pressed close to our mother, who could barely read, and had her read the funny papers over several times to prolong the closeness.

Many children's stories have themes like "Where are you, Mommy?" These stories deal with helplessness, fear of abandonment, and the craving for security. Because these stories help children deal with being in a great big frightening world without much going for them, they want to hear them over and over. Eventually, they memorize the words associated with the pictures and begin to read from memory. We adults act like fools about the level of competence they are displaying, call Mom and Grandma to tell them about the little genius. The children are pleased that we powerful adults are pleased, and they are motivated to master reading and every other task around. Thus, learning and performing at a desirable level grow first out of a caring relationship with a parent.

Children notice that parents start at the corner of the page and read from left to right, from the top down, and that they exclaim in certain ways. All of these observations provide them with pre-reading skills. With attention to letters, sounds, words, and sentences, some learn to read before going to school or are prepared to learn to read when they enter school.

A vivid memory of the beauty of the parent as teacher sticks out in my mind. A three-year-old peeked his head out of the open window of his car and asked his mother, who was filling the tank with gas, what she was doing. She explained that she was giving the car some breakfast, just as he had had breakfast a short while ago. She went on to explain how food provides the energy he needs to run and play, just as gas provides the energy the car needs to run. You could almost see the child's brain turning as he listened intently and pondered the lesson. Because she so intentionally passed on higher-order thinking skills in that little exchange, I asked if she was a teacher. She replied, "No, just a mom." How could this process have been different? The child could have simply been told "I'm getting gas" or, worse, "Close that window and don't bother me."

I witnessed another youngster about the same age who strayed from the checkout counter at a store, stepped on the electronic mat that opened the door nearby, and jumped back in alarm. She looked in amazement, apparently formed the hypothesis that the door and mat were related in some way, and began to test it by stepping on and off the mat. Her mother noted the experimentation, recognized it as a learning opportunity, and began to raise questions and give explanations about how it worked. The little girl walked out of the store with her mother, smiling, arms swinging in the joy of discovery. These little revelations create competence and confidence that foster success in future tasks.

An academic colleague told me of the great pleasure his twenty-month-old gains from deliberately playing a game by his own rules, even though he knows the way it is supposed to be played—showing that the thrust for autonomy and control is innate. Another told of his four-year-old spelling a word and requiring him to say it as he had asked the child in the past. Who is in charge, anyway?

Learning also comes from negative experiences. A three-year-old, furious with her seven-year-old brother, who had been teasing her, grabbed a carving knife off the table and started toward him. Her father caught and held her, calmed her down, and explained in a firm but nonpunitive and nonjudgmental way that such behavior was wrong and would not be allowed, ever! Father, daughter, and son talked about better ways to get along and how to handle disputes.

Young children scream, bite, scratch, and do whatever is necessary to manage fear and insecurity of all kinds—from hunger and abandonment to big brothers who bother them. The aggressive energy of the would-be knifer was not bad or immoral; it was not even deep anger or hatred. Aggressive energy is required for human survival. But it needs modification and management in civilized societies. The father protected the child from her own destructive impulse. By taking the matter seriously and helping the children to discuss appropriate behavior, he encouraged self-control and constructive problem solving. By seeing a child as in need of help—not a demon—he minimized the likelihood of defensive resentment, the repression of a necessary level of assertiveness, and harmful feelings about self.

As cute as they are, babies are not civilized. Indeed, they have murderous potentials. They do not know the drill or have the skills to play the game of life. They will hit and ignore rules to meet their own needs. For instance, I saw a three-year-old go to the head of a line for the airplane toilet. His father explained that he had to wait his turn. Similar explanations must be given over and over.

Socializing children is a long, tough journey, but somebody has to do it. For this reason, it is important for children to be born into a family in which they are wanted. And parents must have the resources and skills to help their children develop.

The willingness and ability of adults to promote development are influenced greatly by their own life experiences. Parents with a reasonable hope of a stable job are usually best able to manage the child-rearing task. The parents of the three-year-old would-be knifer were well educated and employed. The successful and secure fathers mentioned above could take great pleasure in the autonomy, identity, and control efforts of their children as the children gained power and confidence. Even among people without a reasonable chance of a decent job, some find security and skill through religion or in other ways.

But parents under economic, social, and psychological stress—parents with less access to opportunities—more often have difficulties with children. Despite good intentions and sometimes remarkable efforts, their care of children more often ranges from marginal to abusive. "I am" starts here, too (Solnit, Nordhaus, and Lord, 1992). Sustained bad care eventually leads to a deep-seated inner sense of insecurity and inadequacy, emotional pain, and a troublesome sense of self. I observed a nine-year-old child at an airport who had accompanied his mother and siblings to welcome a relative home. In the bright spirit of inquiry, maybe teasing because he knew better, he wondered aloud what would happen if he told the guards at the metal detector that he had a gun. His mother angrily said, "Shut up, or I'll smack you in the mouth." The look of curiosity and fun fell, and he moved to the back of the group, crushed. There was no patient lesson about appropriate time and place or harmful consequences. The child just got put down and controlled.

In the office of my optometrist in a low-income area, a very large woman tried to get her bright-eyed, playful, provocative son to sit in his chair. He was humming, exploring, enjoying himself. He maneuvered just outside the range of her chair. But when he moved too close, in a flash, she snatched him and slapped him to the ground with one powerful blow. Shocked and angered, I almost violated my rule that I not wear my professional hat in public. The doctor told me that the woman had been his patient since childhood. He told me of the abuse and anger she had endured as a child and was inflicting, in turn, on her child. The mother clearly did not have high expectations for her child. But to my eyes, this was a smart little rascal. For reasons that have nothing to do with intelligence, punitive behavior is the more frequent approach of less-educated people. Again, the problem is culturally based.

Part of our religious heritage is the belief that the individual is born bad and is not capable of desirable behavior without punishment, control, and, some believe, redemption. Others view lack of self-control as unnatural and willful. Parents and other authority figures impose control, but external control does not help the young person gain inner or personal control.

An example of this widespread belief can be seen in a former neighbor of mine, who was working as a guard in a high school. When she was told that I had written an article saying it was not necessary to spank children and that I did not spank my own children, she responded, "Oh, I know that's not true. He was my neighbor, and I knew his children. They were very good children."

Relying on punishment and control rather than discussion and support for responsible behavior tends to limit the exploration of ideas and independent thinking. Young people who can't examine ideas may be misled by opportunists and hatemongers. The capacity for independent thinking can best be developed in a child-rearing process that promotes inner control. It requires a gradual allowance of greater freedom and participation in decision making for children as they demonstrate their ability to make good decisions and manage increased freedom responsibly.

The outcomes of the different expectations and child-rearing styles are predictable. The father quizzed by his four-year-old daughter told how her pediatrician had examined her motor control when she was three years old by asking her to write her name in his book and having her read to him. Given the quality of the child-rearing experience she was receiving, he assumed that she might already be able to do so. The child's mother, a teacher in a low-income community, told of a seven-year-old in her school who had not mastered his ABC's, but his mother could not see that she should be concerned. The child was able, but had not had the preparation needed. And that youngster who was slammed to the floor in the eye doctor's office, though intelligent, is having serious behavior and learning problems in school.

My colleagues are academics, and our children grow up surrounded by books, discussions, artistic interests and expressions. We provide a home experience that gives our children the skills they will need in school, as do many families of business and professional people. Many less affluent or less educated families also give their children a rich experience at home. And even when the preschool preparation is not rich, many children's experience puts them above the threshold needed to perform adequately. In a good school, some will excel. But too many schools can't help the underdeveloped.

The Family in the Three Networks

Parents are the carriers of the culture of the networks to which they feel attachment. When they are not part of the mainstream culture, the traditions in these networks can be very different, yet just as meaningful and influential. As parents care for their children, they pass on this culture.

We underestimate the force of the process. Children are in a powerless state in which knowledge and security come from people to whom they are strongly attached emotionally. It takes an unusual effort for a child to be different from the surrounding people and culture. For these reasons, immediate networks greatly affect the future performance of the developing child.

This is particularly the case when opportunities to enter the mainstream culture appear blocked. When an outsider has nobody to identify with, it is difficult to connect. That is why some of the students I grew up with did well in school but not after graduation.

My working-class family was poor and low-status in the steel mill town I grew up in the 1950s, but still was mainstream. The same was true of our Baptist church. There were models of non-mainstream cultural behaviors all around as well. Participation in both was possible for me. But a time came when nonmainstream activities precluded participation in the mainstream. That's when parental standards and expectations and my own emerging personal ones came to the fore.

When I displayed certain behavior, my mother would say, "You can't do that. You are a Comer." Being a Comer meant having mainstream aspirations, without disparaging those who did not. It meant not doing things that were illegal, not engaging in irresponsible sexual behavior.

I remember once when a bare-chested neighbor offered me a cold beer on a hot day, and I declined. We were standing in front of the employment office of the steel mill. My parents knew the personnel officer, and my mother had used this contact to get me and my brothers summer jobs. Beer drinking in public was not acceptable mainstream behavior in the 1950s. It could influence future employment, particularly in hard times, when hard choices are made. Yet that evening, I had a beer with that same neighbor in his home. Kin and friend can live next door or even in the same house but identify with different cultures.

Actually, I had learned this lesson much earlier. When I was eleven, I was about to "liberate" a magazine in the neighborhood drugstore. Suddenly, I looked up and saw I was being observed by a high school friend. My brothers and I played basketball with his younger brother in his family's indoor gym. My mother had worked as a domestic in that home also. If I could steal in the store, I could do it in their home. The magazine remained where it was.

On another occasion, when an opportunity to have sex was offered, I left because it was after my curfew and I knew my father would be out looking for me. I met him on my way home. He did not ask what I was up to. But as he did with all suspicious infractions, he reminded me that if I wanted to be respected and achieve my goals, there were some things I just could not do.

My father's method is important to note. He did not scold or punish. He helped me become responsible for my own good behavior. And every storekeeper, neighbor, or teacher would contact my parents if my behavior was not acceptable. The concerns of my parents and the immediate community were demonstrations of love. It is this concern that promotes honesty, decency, motivation to achieve, and self-reliance.

The Child and the Second Network

By school age, or five years, good child rearing should have led to significant thought and language development, and to desirable social skills, ethical foundations, and emotional development.

During the next period, between five and twelve years, young people should develop a desire to bring tasks to completion. They should gradually become able to manage their aggressive and sexual impulses in acceptable ways. Learning should become both a habit and a passion, channeling much aggressive energy that otherwise can lead to behavior problems, undermining competence and confidence in the following period—a time already complicated by puberty around age twelve.

For most mainstream children, meeting these tasks through the school is simply a continuation of a process begun at home. For students from families marginal to the mainstream culture, this stage is fraught with pitfalls. Lacking home experiences that prepare them to meet the expectations of the school, some children are made anxious by the challenges of these tasks. When they don't experience success, they feel frustrated and, as a result, sometimes act up in troublesome ways. Many eventually drop out of school or perform far below their potential.

Many children have learned to fight because they have not been taught to negotiate for what they want. Some have been told that they will get a beating at home if they don't fight when they are challenged—a catch-22 that only gets them into trouble at school. Teachers too often punish them and hold low expectations for them rather than help them grow along developmental pathways where most mainstream parents have led their children before school.

Unprepared but otherwise good children respond to punishment by fighting back, particularly when the relationship between the teacher and child is not positive. They fight for power and control through teasing and provocation, just as mainstream children do. The struggle is for the same prize—autonomy and identity. The usual response at school is to clamp down on the children. Most parents—because they view their role as protectors and because children are extensions of themselves—will support their children. A teacher and school versus child and parent face-off ensues, eventually creating difficulties for all involved.

In such struggles, children sometimes gain mastery of skills that are self-defeating in the long run, such as manipulation, dishonesty, and ignoring the rights of others. I have seen extreme situations in which children won the power struggle with ineffective parents, then, unprotected, became frightened by their own dangerous impulses and eventually became psychotic.

Some children respond in an opposite way: self-doubt grows, and they give up and withdraw. Afraid to take risks, they shun the mental exploration they need for academic achievement. These students are often neglected while teachers attend to more vociferous kids. If they are as timid socially as academically, they are also neglected by their peers, increasing their sense of isolation. Yet some of the same children can be very active and successful on the playground, in the community, and, eventually, in a gang or any situation they feel comfortable in. They have merely been turned off by school.

These children are still in the north woods, without a map, survival skills, or tools. Most will not continue to develop so as to achieve their social and academic potential. Most go on a downhill course and repeat the marginal experience of their parents, despite the fact that almost all parents want their children to succeed in school and in life.

When are the first signs of this disillusionment?

Because children are children and want adult approval, most of these underprepared students do not immediately challenge the teacher or reject the school program. They come to school lagging in their development compared with mainstream children, but begin to make attachments to teachers and school. They begin to develop and learn. But several factors contribute to their leveling off around the third or fourth grade.

This is when the academic demands of the school begin to outpace the preschool and early school development of many children. The child who was helped to think about the similarity between gas and food is well into a higher order of thinking by this time. The child who was knocked to the floor, who possibly had the same intellectual potential, has very likely not developed abstract thinking and other higher-order skills. He probably can't read or handle numbers very well. But reading and arithmetic are the key to future school and work success.

Also, at this time, children begin to place themselves in the scheme of things—who and what they are, what's possible and what's not. For example, I knew an eight-year-old who heard a fire engine and declared that he wanted to be a fireman. His father discussed what being a fireman was about, but did not disparage the idea. Four years later, when the youngster brought home a brochure outlining the kind of academic program that was required for various careers, the father said, "Let's see what kind of courses you will need to become a fireman." The youngster looked at him as if he had lost his mind. Being a fireman is a respectable position. But the youngster's self-assessment had reached the point where he had entirely different career expectations.

Children who are not doing well in school or whose families are not well connected to the mainstream view themselves as different from those in it—their teachers and fellow students with higher levels of achievement. When called on to achieve, they are being asked, in a very real sense, to be different from their parents and their own network culture. This eventually becomes a serious identity problem that must be worked through if they are to move into the mainstream culture.

Another developmental phenomenon greatly affects performance of children from all backgrounds. As young people seek belonging beyond their family, their group becomes a significant factor. This is a special challenge for children and families from groups that are scapegoated in a society. From the age when a child can be taught to value his difference—say, two or three—parents should help their children identify with truly positive aspects of their group and to understand and manage outside antagonisms. Otherwise, they risk internalizing the negative message—inferior intelligence, criminal, irresponsible—that they will pick up from many sources. My parents provided the positive message, and yet it was almost not enough to protect me from antagonisms in college when I was beyond the protective networks of home, local school, and church community. Some young people attempt to detoxify the negative by adopting those very attitudes and behaviors as an expression of their racial identity—and by rejecting all mainstream attitudes, language, activities, and people. While this response is intended to be protective, it can create patterns of academic and behavioral deficiency that only lead to a sense of powerlessness and victimization rather than effective coping.

I was pleased to see basketball superstar Michael Jordan as the superhero in the film *Space Jam* in a theater full of kids of all backgrounds. It is a long way from *Little Eight Ball,* the depiction of a not-too-smart black kid with a billiard-ball head that was the cartoon I had to watch at the movies. But a full and plentiful range of positive African American images is still missing. Confidence, competence, attachment to mainstream people and activities can be permanently limited without such images and good support for development.

Yet some studies show that 85 percent of black parents never talk about racial identity with their children. When race is mentioned, it is often in angry responses to unfair situations or in extreme efforts to establish positive identity. Sometimes race as a problem is denied in order to reduce discomfort. A white colleague reported that black parents she interviewed initially denied any racial problems in their immediate lives, but after trust was established, they pointed to numerous such problems.

Also, belonging requires living up to peer (particularly clique and gang) expectations. Students who are frustrated and losing confidence are more likely to be involved with peer groups that do not value academic learning and in which they can experience belonging by engaging in behavior that is provocative.

Both the children who make waves and the ones who withdraw become candidates for problem behaviors of all kinds. Insecurities and fears that lead to smoking, drug use, depression, violence, vandalism, early sexual involvement, and pregnancy have some roots in early school difficulties. School difficulties and unmet needs—particularly a sense of belonging—contribute to gang membership.

Some student misbehavior is simply a tactic to drive people away so that they won't discover learning problems. That was the case when I was asked to see a fourth-grade student who was hostile and would not do his work. He was using the hostility to cover up the fact that he could not read.

When enough students are not succeeding in a school, a negative environment generates and reinforces bad behavior, despite the fact that most students would like better conditions. Students doing well academically are more likely to become a part of peer groups that support desirable social performance. This is the case even in difficult school environments. Nonetheless, in high-stress areas, more severe conditions operate to limit preteen achievement.

The Adolescent in the Second Network

Adolescence, increasingly since midcentury, has become a special challenge for all. The body and mind are changing rapidly, howling for independence and self-expression in and beyond the family. But the reality for most adolescents is continued dependence on parents and limited opportunities for self-expression. Most have not had the experiences or acquired the judgment that will enable them to handle the complexities of this age. That is why an intelligent child can do the dumbest things.

While a teenager longs for independence from the family, the thought of it is also frightening. But such fear is unacceptable, so it is covered up by denial and bravado, exaggerated pressure for independence, and a pose of invincibility that can lead to trouble. The predicament of the adolescent requires a reduction in size of the parent, often taking the form of verbal attacks, belittling judgment, resisting advice.

When I was a teenager, a policeman who was a family friend stopped me outside a dangerous dive and advised me not to go in. I politely thanked him for his advice. As soon as he left, I went in to see what it was that these adults were trying to keep me away from. In East Chicago in the 1950s, that was not a problematic decision. In East Chicago and many other places in the 1990s, it could turn out to be troublesome indeed.

The behavior is no less challenging to parents and teachers. Provocative moves to gain power at this age can seem more like insolence than they did when children were younger. Teenage delight in new gains often comes at a time when many parents feel a loss of their edge. I remember that it took a lot for me to be happy when my thirteen-year-old son beat me in a billiards game for the first time, even though I had been promising him that his time would come. Was I—protector, provider, leader—slowing down? Was my charge overtaking me?

Teachers and parents who understand the turmoil and are secure enough themselves can go with the flow. They don't take the attacks on themselves personally. In ways that work best for each individual, they provide support and maintain desirable standards by cajoling, encouraging, paying attention, being available. They support as much independence as the young persons can manage in a responsible way—but won't hesitate to reduce it when they can't manage it, while promising greater independence again when they can.

Such parents and teachers are promoting inner control, motivation, direction, and responsibility for self and concern for others. This is very important today with all the new technological developments. Because information often comes from TV, the Internet, or other outside sources rather than from parents, teachers, or close community people, young persons must be prepared to understand their world and, without parental presence, do the right thing. They must be ready to meet their own needs and avoid exploitation of and by others.

Parenting is tough work, and some parents don't have adequate resources and support. We are all busy. So some parents listen to

"I don't need you" and just retreat. They let the school or somebody else attend to their teenagers. But children need parents more than ever during adolescence. They say "go away," but they don't mean far away. They just need a little extra space. More than a few teens have resisted negative peer pressure with "My mother would kill me if I did that."

Nonetheless, many parents do retreat when their children need them the most, even in affluent areas. It is difficult to get a parking space on parent night at school during the elementary years. Parking space is no problem in middle school. By high school, the parking lot is almost empty.

It is more difficult for parents under economic and social stress to go with the flow and to hang in there all the way. As a society, we have done very little to address the special challenge of adolescence. For many mainstream young people, activities that support desirable development are built into the family and school life. This is the age, before the adolescent can drive, when parents carpool them almost nonstop from swimming to drama to music lessons. Most successful elite schools pay great attention to activities that allow student expression. Some youth activities are tied to private religious and social organizations. Family business and vacation activities expose mainstream young people to experiences that promote their development.

Less is provided for nonmainstream young people. Many believe that volunteer organizations should do this. And they try, but even here there is much more available for mainstream middle-income young people. I co-chaired the Carnegie Corporation Task Force on Youth Development and Community Programs with Wilma Tisch, a prominent community organization leader. Our report, *A Matter of Time: Risk and Opportunity in the Nonschool Hours,* was released in 1992. We found there are more than 17,000 national and local youth organizations in the United States—large national and local bootstrap operations; religious, ethnic, and racial group organizations; sports, museums, public libraries, park and recreation organizations; adult service groups. The report was based on extensive interviews with young people, organization leaders, research papers, and site visits. We found that young people need and want these programs. The report states:

> Community organizations provide mentors, adults who have time to talk, to listen, and to provide mature guidance . . . facilities that provide safe havens for youth . . . approaches that foster adolescents' competence and life skills . . . often focused on the challenges of sexuality, alternatives to violence, and prevention of alcohol, tobacco and other drug use . . . opportunities for youth to be involved in community service, to address local problems, and to participate in the decisions of youth organizations . . . opportunities for public performances, rites and symbols of recognition, and reflection with others on personal and group accomplishments. [Carnegie Council on Adolescent Development, 1992]

The volunteers and paid workers do a remarkable, even heroic job. But they are even less appreciated than schoolteachers. And these organizations are not adequately funded. Stability and continuity are often not possible under these circumstances. Adult workers are not given the kind of training and support they need. Because we don't think in terms of personal development, these programs are generally not tied to schools and parents to create the kind of seamless web of support for development that existed for many in the past. And most troubling, they usually are not able to reach the young people living under the greatest economic and social stress.

Much of what teenagers do in the way of recreation does not support their development. In no activity that young people are involved in—private or public school, religious or secular, after-school, media—do we give them adequate, systematic preparation to become responsible citizens in an open, democratic society.

Too much television consumes the out-of-school time of too many young people of all ages: about 21 percent of the waking hours of mostly unsupervised young people between nine and fourteen. By way of comparison, they spend only 31 percent of their nonsleep time in school. The amount of violence on television has become a matter of national concern. But the paucity of constructive role models and the plethora of undesirable behaviors they observe is probably more worrisome. And where community and family functioning deteriorate, the impact of television behavior burgeons. Most talk shows and other media genres focus on the extremes, which are often viewed by young people as the norm. Thus, young people have unacceptable behavior on parade without counsel of adults and responsible peers—and too many will imitate it.

A court worker in the Midwest told me a tragic story. A young teen in her custody shot and killed a friend and could not understand why the dead youngster did not get up. His ability to understand reality had not developed as quickly as his ability to act.

Am I making too much of what goes on in adolescence? I think not. What the young person experiences here will have a profound influence on the rest of life. For instance, I was so poorly coordinated until I was about thirteen years old that the outfielders in our gym class softball games would sit in the infield when I came up to bat. But suddenly things changed, and I hit a line drive that rolled all the way to the track around the field. Even now—probably when self-doubt arises—I think of that left fielder chasing the ball as I rounded third base, and I smile.

The academic, athletic, artistic, and social problems and successes of this period provide the critical competence and confidence that make mainstream participation a realistic possibility or not. It is a time when identity, discipline, and habit patterns are established in a positive or precarious way. Adult success rests heavily on the platform put in place here.

I have emphasized adolescence here as critically important, but it builds on the successful transition from home to school that takes place between the ages of three and ten. And the experiences of the first three years of life, in particular, are what make it possible for children to be ready to learn. We must pay attention to child development from birth onward. When we wait until there's teenage pregnancy, drug use, and violence and then ask what happened, we are missing the boat by a decade or more.

The Third Network

The way policies and practices established by business, political, and other leaders (the third network) impact the secondary and family networks can be illustrated by the changes in my hometown, East Chicago, Indiana. A former college classmate recently recalled that in the 1950s, this industrial city of about 50,000 people, then about 25 percent black, produced a large number of black students who were very successful at Indiana University. Three made Phi Beta Kappa in a four-year span; many were honor roll and professional school graduates. Our African American social fraternity was first among all fraternities in academic honors for two years and near the top for about five.

Such achievement had not occurred before and has not occurred since. In the early 1950s, there were still enough jobs so that most people had enough money to pay for basic family needs. There was little community and family deterioration, and people of all economic groups attended the same schools, which were adequately supported. Though the teachers were all white, by the 1950s, most were fair and encouraged all students to achieve.

The church-based mainstream black culture, which highly valued education, was still dominant. My family and church culture (primary network), like that of similar families, generated the deep-seated sense of belonging, reinforced the values and ways of the larger culture, and connected us to it. Our family was involved in a web of relationships that touched our school and workplace (secondary network) and policymakers (tertiary network) and made them work for us. An example of this is the way my parents' relationship with the employment officer at the steel foundry enabled me to get a job at seventeen, despite its minimum-age policy of eighteen.

Because it was a small city, before much television or long commutes from home to work, there was still a real sense of community. There was almost no random violence. The football game between the two rival high schools was a huge event. With adequate income and opportunity within reach, the city had great vitality. And even poor black kids could feel they had the chance to achieve the American dream.

But by the 1980s, national and international economic policies led to a change in the steel industry, and the Inland Steel plant in the city gradually downsized from a high of 25,000 employees in 1978 to 8,500 today. Since the 1950s, local policymakers have used land zoning, exclusion of low-income housing, and other tactics to keep the people most in need of increased family support services inside the city while moving the most affluent to the surrounding suburbs. Consequently, much business and industry has also moved to these more affluent areas, leaving the neediest communities with weak local tax bases.

These policies affected the secondary or service network—jobs, schools, family services—and, in turn, the primary or family network. Policymakers paid little attention to the question of how to increase successful community and family functioning in the face of technological change. As a result, many families are increasingly unable to afford such basic needs as health and child care. And except for physicians, the people in the areas of human development have educations, salaries, status, and working conditions that are among the least competitive.

The Individual Stands Alone?

All three networks in a society must operate smoothly to create conditions and interactions that will enable families, schools, and community organizations to help children fully develop. The differences in the way the networks operated in the past and operate now is the primary cause of the differences in outcome for various young people and groups.

A positive tone is created in a society through its effort to enable families and children to function well and to sense that they belong. More than laws and punishment, caring leaders and institutions are what influence most people to do what is fair and responsible. The thought of what my parents and associates would think about me and, in turn, of what I would think about myself was what enabled me generally to do the right thing. Although we live in more complex times, the dynamic that contributes most to desirable behavior remains the same. Societies that don't work to promote positive community, child, and family functioning will permit its opposite to take root (Hamburg, 1992).

Children who have a caring developmental experience have a good chance of becoming winners able to meet their adult responsibilities. And children who have a difficult developmental experience have a good chance of becoming losers. The quality of development of my children affects what happens to you and your children, and vice versa. So there is a need for concern among all about all our children.

Some individuals can function adequately even when the three networks of influence work against them during their developmental years. Such people are the American ideal, but they are rare. My mother was such a person. Most of us are what we are by virtue of the support for development we received, our opportunity structure, our own effort, and—very important—good luck. A modern society probably cannot thrive for long with conditions that require exceptional performance from large numbers of people who have not had reasonably adequate developmental experiences.

Contrary to our First Myth, differences in the opportunity structure created by policies and behaviors in all three networks affect outcomes. Mainstream young people are favored in every way, and this failure to support the development of other young people hurts society. Some who are the products of favorable conditions in all three networks feel they made it on their own or are more entitled, anyway. As the myth of intelligence and motivation continues to be passed on from one generation to the next, it becomes more and more difficult to create the opportunity structures needed by all.

In the Club Room of the Ritz-Carlton in Palm Springs, a young man of privilege who looked to be about fifteen years old read a *USA Today* story on social programs and announced grandly, "I am against all social programs." In keeping with my policy of not wearing my professional hat in public, this son of Hugh and Maggie had to leave and take a long walk.

References

Carnegie Council on Adolescent Development. *A Matter of Time: Risk and Opportunity in the Nonschool Hours.* Executive Summary. New York: Carnegie Corporation of New York, 1992.

Hamburg, D. A. *Today's Children: Creating a Future for a Generation in Crisis.* New York: Times Books, 1992.

Solnit, A. J., with B. F. Nordhaus and R. Lord. *When Home Is No Haven: Child Placement Issues.* New Haven, Conn.: Yale University Press, 1992.

So You Want to Work in Schools?

Even today, many people are very glib about what can and should be done in schools. In *Maggie's American Dream*, a book about my family, I share my motivation for wanting to work in underperforming schools serving mostly low-income students. In this chapter, I describe the initial shock I experienced as we encountered school problems in the real world that are more complex and difficult to address than most people, even policymakers, believe. It was sink or swim for us. After a near-death experience, we swam.

I WANTED TO GIVE LOW-INCOME BLACK CHILDREN THE SAME CHANCE in life—through education—that I had had. I wanted to find out why the schools were not working for them and to help make them do so. I was delighted to be assigned two elementary schools, Simeon Baldwin and Martin Luther King Jr. All this was fine in theory, but I was totally unprepared for what happened the first day the students arrived. All hell broke loose.

At Baldwin, three of the fourteen classrooms were totally out of control. Eight were on the edge and could have fallen apart at any moment. Only the three classrooms with veteran teachers were functioning adequately. I went into one of the classrooms and could not believe my eyes and ears. There were a couple of eight-year-olds chasing each other around the room. Two were standing on tables screaming across the room, imitating something they had seen on television. Other children were whining and crying, "Teacher, teacher." One child was walking aimlessly around the room, opening and closing cabinet drawers, dumping paint brushes, pounding erasers, and doing whatever else came to mind with the next thing he encountered. The noise was incredible. Anxious children were sucking their thumbs in an effort to find comfort.

The shaken teacher called for order. The children ignored her. I called for order in my most firm and assertive way. They hesitated a second and then ignored me. That had never happened to me before with children. Mrs. Brown, assistant to the principal for administration, arrived. She was a black woman, a senior teacher, and one of the three people in the project who had been in the school the year before. She knew the children and their parents, and she was able to get them to quiet down. But the problem was far from over. She couldn't stay there and teach.

I retreated to the hallway. One of the children who had been crying followed me out the door. I noticed that he was behind me as I started up the stairs. He was scared and held out his arms. I instinctively embraced him to give comfort, but also to receive it. I was almost as frightened as he was. As he sobbed, his small body trembled against mine. I thought to myself, "Kid, what are we doing to you?"

One part of me said, "What am I doing here?" and wanted to run. The other part of me said, "You want to make a difference—and this is your chance."

It was 1968, and I was director of the Yale Child Study Center team in a collaborative school intervention project with the New Haven school system. Baldwin and King schools were a subsystem in which our team—a social worker, psychologist, special education teacher—was to develop a way of working that would be applied to the entire school system. We were to work with a principal for administration and a principal for instruction. The strategy was for our team to work in two schools for a year and then, working with school people and parents, apply our child development and behavior knowledge to improve the schools.

We were in trouble; I could see that. We adults had to set clear expectations for the children, I decided. I made this point at an emergency meeting of the program leaders. I suggested we hold assemblies and orient the children to these expectations. Everybody was in agreement except the principal for instruction. He felt that this was heavy-handed adult control of children.

A half dozen teachers expressed the same attitude. Lining up before and after school, walking the children to the toilets, and other order-producing devices were adult conspiracies to repress the young, their spirit, freedom, need for creative expression, and so on. One teacher likened our plans to the abuse of blacks in the South and the Holocaust. I couldn't believe my ears. But it was clear to me that in addition to a difference in concepts about how children develop and learn, a struggle for power was going on.

The principal for instruction was an advocate of open classroom, a good but often misused concept. (It is a student-centered design with less structure, both physical and instructional. It works best with experienced and skilled teachers. Most of our teachers lacked experience.) Several teachers were his recent students, and several others were interns under his supervision who had not taught before. The open-classroom approach was described as especially useful for black children—victims of the effects of oppression and abuse passed down from generation to generation for three hundred years. Open classrooms would free them and allow them to benefit from their heretofore repressed intelligence. Teaching was to be lively and exciting—a happening. Learning was to be through exploration and discovery, to be as spontaneous as possible.

In an effort to be cooperative, I gave in to the pressure of the principal for instruction. Our views weren't that far apart. I believe that exploration and discovery are important ways children learn, but within a framework of structure. The teachers argued that the problems would go away, that each teacher, not the leadership, had to take responsibility for establishing order. They said that the real problems were administrative: they lacked supplies; some rooms were too large, some too small; some had too many children; and so on.

Most of the teachers were young and white. Excluding the three experienced teachers, the average teaching experience was one year. Three had no previous experience at all. But they were idealistic and enthusiastic. They were out to do better by black people and black children than their parents. They were convinced that black children could do as well as anybody else, and they were going to prove it.

After the emergency meeting, the administrators scurried around, trying to get the teachers the things they said they needed. Some of the teachers did provide their children with more struc-ture, but most of the open-classroom teachers did not. We soon heard rumors that the parents and the people in the neighborhood were furious and planned to march on the school. That would have destroyed us—a thirty-second television spot, an embarrassed super-intendent and central administration, an outraged school board, an angry alderman, and program termination. Wendy Winters, our social worker, was able to talk with a few parents, and I was able to get a community leader to speak with a couple. Instead of marching on the school, they sent a delegation. Boy, were they angry!

There were nine people in the group. They went in to see Mrs. Brown. I heard one person say, "Where is this person from Yale?" Mrs. Brown liked me and tried to protect me, but the parents wanted Yale. Yale had a town-gown problem with all of New Haven, a more serious problem with the black community, and an impos-sible problem with the low-income black community. In the latter, it was known as an institution of great prestige and closed doors. It was believed that its only interest in the low-income neighborhoods around it was to do research. Ironically, the burden of being Yale fell on Hugh and Maggie Comer's son, Jimmy.

When I entered the room, it appeared to me that although the women might have known that I was black, Mr. Best, their leader, had not known. He was a clear-thinking, articulate, forceful man. He stated the parents' concerns directly and succinctly—but with the realization that I was black, some of the anger went out of his voice.

The problem was the usual—promises, promises from the school system and Yale. The schools were to have had experienced teachers, leadership that would give as much time to instruction as to administration, extra money for planning time, participation in program development by parents, and so on. The promises were not kept, and the changes made were not working.

I pointed out to the parents that I had been involved in only a small part of the planning and that it was my impression that things weren't going well because there hadn't been the kind of planning that was promised. "If you'll give me a chance, it will happen."

They looked at each other and arrived at a consensus without saying a word. Mr. Best turned to me and said, "Okay, we're going to hold you responsible." My being black bought us time, but only "five minutes." They were more interested in results than race.

Now I really had a problem. Within a week of starting, I was being held responsible for making the program work—without official authority or any previous experience in applying the principles of child development and behavior to a school.

5

My Work

While my book Waiting for a Miracle *considers the school as a system within interacting systems, this chapter describes how we worked initially with pilot school staff, parents, and students to create a model that turned dysfunctional, low-achieving schools into well-functioning, high-achieving schools and then disseminated the model widely. Many of the methods and principles we piloted in the 1960s and 1970s are common school practices today, but often without the intentional focus on student development and staff preparation that is needed.*

ON REFLECTION, IT IS NOT SURPRISING THAT MY QUESTIONS ABOUT the life performance of people should lead me to my work in education. Our schools are simultaneously a microcosm and a reflection of the larger society. They offer clues about what makes the society run well or badly. On the other hand, because schools are greatly influenced by what is going on in the society, improving them in any significant way inevitably requires improving the society.

I recently visited a school in the Midwest that has been implementing our School Development Program for five years. It is a wonderfully warm place, and most of the students have passed the state proficiency test despite the fact that it is not a magnet school and the children are not categorized as gifted.

Looking in on a fifth-grade graduation in an auditorium full of parents, I was struck by the applause for one student in particular,

Natasha. Later, her mother and the principal hugged warmly in the hall and both laughed about how far they had come in their relationship. Afterward, the principal told me that the mother was referring to their initial meeting. Her son Timmy had called his teacher a motherfucker. The mother, summoned to the school and told what Timmy had said, knocked him to the floor while calling him a motherfucker!

It took a lot of work to develop the relationship the family and the school enjoyed on that happy graduation day; it took non-judgmental and respectful getting-to-know-each-other meetings between the family and the school people, cajoling, guiding, advising, explaining, and holding high expectations. The family still has its rough edges, but the applause for Natasha represented the whole school cheering them on.

I see school people throughout the country applying what our Yale Child Study Center team learned from trying to change two New Haven schools. The way in which schools support children like Natasha and Timmy and their families is an outgrowth of what I learned by helping a boy named Johnny.

During the first year, the "bad boy" of one of the schools, Johnny, was everybody's project. A year later, with the support of the school, he was behaving much better. But one day, he began fighting in the hallway. After several teachers stopped the fight, one of them, now understanding that kids act out their feelings, said, "I wonder what's going on with him." The year before, the comment probably would have been, "That bad Johnny Jones is at it again. How does anyone expect us to teach when we have to put up with kids like that?"

Back in his classroom, the child knocked over his desk. His teacher hurried into the room, but instead of sending him to the principal for punishment, she said, "Johnny, what's the matter? What's going on?" He paused and began to cry. His father was in jail, and the youngster had been eagerly awaiting his return on a Christmas pass. Something had happened, and the pass had been withdrawn. The youngster was devastated.

The teacher told Johnny that she understood how disappointed he must be, but that taking his feelings out on other people only made matters worse. She helped him write a letter to his father expressing his disappointment, recognizing his father's disappointment, and telling him how he would be looking forward to the time when he was able to come home. Now instead of being hurt and helpless, Johnny was empowered. The school became a supportive place. Johnny's academic and social performance would continue to improve greatly.

When we began our work in 1968, many educators believed a child either had ability and was motivated or didn't. If the student did poorly, it was his fault, nobody else's. More generous assessments by behavior professionals focused on an underachieving child's intellectual, psychological, and social impairments, but still the focus was limited to the child and, at most, his or her family and community. While my childhood experiences had told me that school performance was determined by more than that, when we began our work, I was not sure what else was operating. The only way to find out was to learn about a couple of schools. Then we could try to change them so that they would work better for the students (Cohen and Solnit, 1996).

I held an appointment as assistant professor of psychiatry at the Yale Child Study Center, a part of the Yale University School of Medicine. The YCSC team that I directed was involved in a joint effort with the New Haven school system. The team consisted of a social worker, a psychologist, a special education teacher, and myself. The New Haven school system component was led by Samuel Nash, their director of special services. Our initial YCSC intervention team was designed to include people already at schools so that once we learned how to make schools work, districts could use existing staff and the cost would not be unreasonable.

The idea was to have two elementary schools, Simeon Baldwin (kindergarten–sixth grade) and Martin Luther King Jr. (kindergarten–fourth grade), serve as representatives of the entire system so that we could intervene, learn, and apply our findings systemwide and beyond. The strategy we outlined in our proposal for funding from the Ford Foundation was for us to *become an integral part* of the two schools rather than impose intervention on them. With staff and parents, we would begin to bring about comprehensive change.

We quickly learned that change is not easy. In fact, our start was so rocky that the parents almost threw us out. Even at the end of five years, we had to leave Baldwin School rather than fight a principal. (We replaced Baldwin with a school that had a similar profile, Katherine Brennan Elementary School.) But without a willingness to change everything and everybody in the school's social system—not only the students—important opportunities are overlooked. Research that concentrates only on isolated aspects of schooling tells you very little.

Three years passed before we had a good school climate and seven years before we had significant academic improvement. Ninety-nine percent of the students at the two schools were black, and more than 70 percent were on welfare. They had been the lowest-achieving groups in the city's thirty-three schools, and by the fourth grade were eighteen and nineteen months behind in mathematics and language arts respectively. By 1984, sixteen years later, the two schools were tied for the third and fourth highest levels of achievement in the city on nationally standardized tests and had the best attendance in the city. Serious behavior problems had been eliminated (Comer, 1988).

The School Development Program's Evolution

Today, the School Development Program (SDP) is a child-focused, data-directed process at work in more than 650 schools in twenty-eight states. As I describe its evolution, it may sound as if we knew what we were doing from the beginning. We didn't. Initially, the project was just trying to survive. We began our work with a theoretical understanding that it was important to involve parents, community members, teachers, psychologists, social workers, and noninstructional staff members (the stakeholders) in the process of school improvement. But we did not know how to do it.

We did know that through positive bonding between the teacher and pupil, desirable child development could take place, and we believed that with good development, the students would learn. But the traditional school does not lend itself to strong positive bonding; teachers teach what they are told to teach, and students are expected to learn—if they are able. There is too little opportunity to engage students and to arouse and extend their curiosity so that they can develop a passion for learning.

We learned very quickly that nobody was deliberately a bad guy. But bad things were happening to the children. The parents, staff, and students wanted to succeed, but some of the students were poorly prepared for the learning process of school, and the staff didn't have the training to be able to close the gap. The traditional schooling was not based on what is known about how children develop and learn. It was mechanical, with no attention paid to the interactions of the human beings, small and large, who were involved.

Traditional schools are hierarchical and authoritarian in a way that does not encourage staff cooperation. Instead of promoting a sense of ownership and shared responsibility for outcomes, such management promotes isolation or clique formation, blame casting, and defensiveness. Every difference can become a flash point—religion, race, educational level, prestige of teacher's alma mater, professional task within the school, pedagogical and child-rearing philosophies. During our first year, we had sharp differences in all these areas. Adults and children struggled for power and security with much finger pointing, blaming, and student fighting.

The most vulnerable staff and parents and, particularly, students were victimized regularly. Every impairment—physical, psychological, social, intellectual—set up a student for victimization. While staff could quit or transfer and parents could stay away from the school, the students had to attend. And they got blamed for the effects of the dysfunctional school environment: "These kids can't learn."

Some students can learn in difficult circumstances when they receive strong support from parents or others outside the school. And a rare few can learn well under any conditions. But most students will not develop and achieve well in difficult school communities.

In short, the traditional was not working. But neither did our initial efforts.

We learned that formal lectures about child development and behavior are of minimal benefit. Some of the teachers who most agreed with the *ideas* could not apply them in the classroom. One wanted to be a friend to the point that she lost her authority and her ability to help her students grow. Teacher autonomy in the instruction and curriculum areas didn't work. Some could develop instruction that was age-appropriate and that stimulated growth and learning, but too many could not. And there was no schoolwide plan they could act from. Nobody, in or outside the schools, could just make improvement take place.

Through trial and error, we began to bring about the thinking, planning, and changes that evolved into the nine critical components of our present-day SDP. Eventually, the stakeholders organized themselves into three teams—planning and management, mental health, and a parent group. But without well-developed management skills, school-based management teams can interact badly. To aid their work, we identified three operations or primary activities. And to prevent difficult interactions, we eventually agreed on guiding principles—again, three—that allowed everybody to work well together.

Let's start by looking at the three teams (see Figure 5.1).

The School Planning and Management Team (SPMT) creates the vision for where the school wants to go. Teachers, instead of working on their own, profit from schoolwide collaborative planning that addresses the needs of the entire school community. Each SPMT creates a comprehensive plan designed to achieve its vision and to identify and make best use of the resources already in the school.

We learned during the first years that the optimal composition of such a team is ten to fourteen people selected from and by each major group at the school. The parents select four or five members; the teachers select one representative from each grade level; the nonprofessional staff such as custodian and clerk select a member; the social worker represents the Student and Staff Support Team; and the principal is a member, usually the chair. The team meets at least once a month—usually once a week at the beginning of the year—and also whenever special issues need to be discussed.

Through the SPMT, the schools determine what change is needed and what is possible, at a speed they can manage. The team plans, communicates, and coordinates all of the many things that are going on in the school. It deals with problems or assigns them to subcommittees, and the team members identify and act on opportunities for school improvement. Because the team is representative of all adults involved in the school, all feel ownership and responsibility for the outcomes.

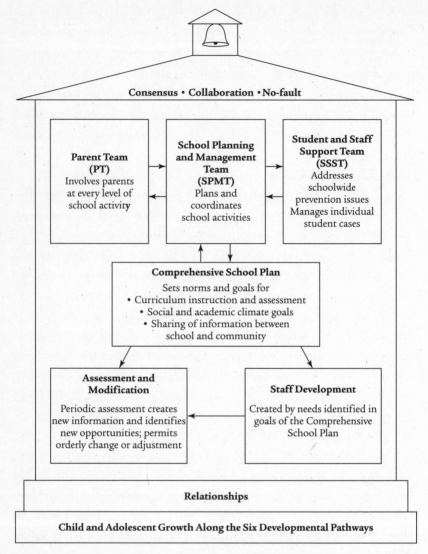

Figure 5.1. Model of the SDP Process

Source: Copyright © 1996 by Teachers College, Columbia University. Reprinted by permission.

During our first years, the Parent Team was made up of people who came to throw us out but stayed to help us build. This team allows parents to share their knowledge about their children and the community with the staff, who in turn share their knowledge about child behavior and learning with the parents. A social worker and, later, a teacher worked with the parents to help them connect with and effectively support teachers and the work of the schools. Teachers and support staff would present academic and child development workshops at coffee klatches planned by and for parents.

Between 1977 and 1980, we had two program components that involved parents deeply in the work of the school. The first was the selection and preparation of a parent to serve as a teacher assistant in each classroom. The second was the Social Skills Curriculum for Inner-City Children project, which helped the students develop skills that children in the mainstream already have simply from growing up in the homes and social networks of their parents.

Working in these ways has created mutual trust and a shared belief in and hope for the students. This approach creates an accountability that can't possibly be matched by rules, penalties, and the few extra dollars that merit pay brings to individual teachers—or pay for parent participation. On the other hand, pay can be useful to poor families and does not create divisiveness.

The Student and Staff Support Team (originally called the Mental Health Team but renamed to avoid pejorative overtones) is made up of the school guidance counselor, special education teacher, nurse, psychologist, social worker, and school-based health clinic representatives. The team helps the staff and the parents to foster desirable behavior in the children. This is done more by changing the culture of the school to better meet the developmental needs of children than by working directly with children. Our chief role is to help the parents and staff to understand that children are not just good or bad, smart or dumb, as their behavior might suggest.

All are born underdeveloped. Some have not mastered the rules of the game and have not had much of a chance to acquire the skills they need. When they are called upon to do what they have not been prepared to do, they may lose confidence. And they may act up.

Parents want their children to be successful, but many parents are themselves unprepared to prepare their children for school. In some cases, economic and social stress make it difficult, even when they know what to do. As a result, too many children come to school prepared for life at the playground, the housing project, and other familiar places, but not prepared for the expectations and demands of the school.

The good news is that by emphasizing child development—as opposed to control and punishment—parents and staff together can promote desirable development and behavior. The way all the teams pull together to benefit the school and the students is demonstrated by the case of a troubled third grader.

This eight-year-old had been traumatized and did not trust adults. She was doing minimal work and would not look at her teacher or smile. At the end of seven months with a caring, reliable, responsible teacher, she finally looked at her and smiled. The teacher, while pleased, was also distressed because in eight weeks she would have to pass the child on and would not be able to build their relationship.

The Mental Health Team held a case conference to discuss this child's needs and experiences and to examine the way continuity and bonding between child and teacher support social and academic growth, while the discontinuity or defective bonding in too many of our students impedes progress. The SPMT was asked to create a subcommittee of staff and of parents selected by the parent team to address this problem.

They came up with a plan for teachers to keep students for two years: first and second, third and fourth. The result was that some children who made no academic gain in the first year made two or more years of gain in the second year. With continuity, trust, and bonding came a willingness to open up and take the risks that academic learning requires. Because all were involved, these gains were a victory for the entire school, and the confidence building had a synergistic effect. "We can do anything. What's next?"

Now that we have seen how the teams work, let's turn to the three operations or primary activities.

The *comprehensive school plan* embodies the SPMT vision in both the social and the academic achievement areas. It uses activities that are common in some schools, like Welcome Back to School potluck suppers, book fairs, fashion shows, field trips to museums and other educational institutions, or producing and selling calendars, to create a good school climate.

Once the schools had their own comprehensive plan, they were no longer forced to appear progressive by accepting every research and mini-intervention program that universities, service clubs, and others proposed—whether it was timely and useful or not. The schools engaged the outside world to help carry out their own plan. In a climate of trust, teachers began to admit that there were areas in which they could use help. This led to the teachers creating their own *staff development plan,* which in turn led to *assessment and modification* of the comprehensive school plan as new needs were identified.

Working together successfully is made possible by three guiding principles:

The no-fault principle: Finger pointing and faultfinding only generate defensiveness. Focusing on ways to prevent and solve problems promotes accountability.

Consensus decision making: Voting can lead to power and personality struggles that have little to do with the needs of children. There are winners, losers, and some who say, "You won; you do it." To reduce clique behavior and personality politics, we discuss what appears to be good for the children, then we go with what most think will work—with the proviso that if it doesn't, we will try the other ideas next. And in the process, a better approach than any previously discussed often turns up.

Collaboration: We agree that the members of the team cannot paralyze the school principal, who has legal authority and responsibility, whether or not he heads the team. But the principal cannot ignore the considered opinions of team members. This promotes a feeling of true collaboration and responsibility for program outcomes.

With the nine elements of the SDP process in place, no teacher has to face difficult problems alone. Teachers begin to share effective practices and to contribute their thoughts to the solution of problems and exploitation of opportunities throughout the school, and all share a sense of pride with each good outcome. And yet each school, acting from the nine elements, addresses its needs in its own way.

The SDP process, when working properly, is like the chain and sprocket of a bicycle. Appropriately assembled, it allows parts that can't take you anywhere separately to be pulled together. Effort applied to the pedals now moves the system, under the control of the cyclist. With a working bike, disparate elements become more effective—curriculum, instruction, assessment, use of technology. Another way to think about it is that it incorporates many small engines of effort, which sometimes work in opposition, into a more powerful and directed engine.

In our first schools, a can-do attitude gradually permeated all activities and interactions. The students now had positive models among the most meaningful people in their lives—parents and teachers. They caught the new spirit and became the carriers of the changed and ultimately desirable school culture. Thus, for example, when someone accidentally stepped on the foot of a new student, the newcomer was ready to fight. But one of his classmates said, "Hey, man, we don't do that in this school." Once he learned that he didn't have to fight his way in, he dropped his fists and also became a carrier.

The students felt comfortable and confident not only about themselves but also about the school around them. They were motivated to achieve more and to behave in a way that won them approval. That is just what had happened for me at home and in school, and for most people who are successful in school.

The makeup of the teams, the operations, the guiding principles that we evolved were based very directly on what we learned as we lived in these initial project schools, observed, and applied our knowledge of child development. The changed way of operating was responsible for the improved outcomes in the schools.

Nobody could mandate change, but collaborative self-change was possible. When staff and parents come to believe in their ability to work in this way, and to believe in the students, they search actively for opportunities to make the school work better. With each success, the staff become more open to the possibility of major changes, observing and learning from children, adjusting their program to help them develop and learn.

While we started with and still work more in elementary schools, the School Development Program is now being used in more than 150 middle and high schools. The same basic nine elements are used. But here, consistent with what we know about child development, the young people themselves are involved in school governance and activity teams. Their opinions are solicited, considered, and, when appropriate, acted upon. While they receive supervision and help in all their activities, the strategy is to give them the level of independence they can manage and hold them accountable. For example, in one middle school, two teachers planning a museum field trip stated their goals for the trip and enlisted the students to develop strategies to achieve those goals, with the teachers providing guidance and participating in the activity.

We now understand that the School Development Program is effective, when properly implemented, for several reasons. It provides a framework, both theoretical and practical, and the kind of structures I have described. It provides tools and skills that teachers often do not receive elsewhere. With these, they are able to systematically carry out processes that promote child development, teaching, and learning. And people with deep knowledge in these areas are available to coach and assist until the changed ways of working are internalized by individuals and schools.

Survival and Funding

In the early years, however, our spread and even our survival were far from assured.

The history of funding for the SDP provides some insight into the difficulty of finding support even for programs with goals as seemingly commendable as ours—to improve the chances of all children and of low-income minority-group children in particular. Issues of race, conflicting theories about how children learn in school, imperfect disseminating of the program, and simple survival were all interrelated.

At the end of the first five years of our pilot work in New Haven, our Ford Foundation project officer recommended continued support. But consultants in psychiatry advised the senior program officer that our model was unworkable. They thought our children had psychological problems that needed to be professionally treated, while our model assumed that most of the children were fine and the system created the problems that needed to be addressed. The foundation's consultants were operating from the one-to-one treatment model—doctor and sick patient—they were used to. We were using an interactive systems model and believed that improvement of school management and climate and relations among students, parents, and staff was essential to good student social and academic performance.

We were not refunded.

Fortunately, the staff and parents had benefited enough from our program to save us. A school social worker, who was preparing to take over when our YCSC team left, decided to refer out for clinical treatment a child with the kind of problems that teachers had been managing themselves with our Mental Health Team support. The teachers marched on the principal and insisted that the social worker not return. Yale Child Study Center and Ford Foundation phase-out funds supported our work until we could find new support.

But finding another source was not easy. While the climate of the schools was greatly improved after five years, the test scores had not moved—although everybody in the schools knew that this was imminent. Indeed, our approach is not specifically designed to improve test scores. It is designed to create conditions that promote student development, adequate teaching, and, in turn, adequate levels of learning.

A description of the change during the first five years, written voluntarily by a data collector just before she left to take another job, was dramatic and compelling. She described how anxious the testing had made the children in the beginning. Some could not sit still. Others would scribble in the areas where they were supposed to supply answers, sometimes pressing the pencil very hard and making dark marks. Some would cry and run out of the room. Four years later, the children were confident, cooperative, and able to concentrate on the task and respond to the questions. But they did not yet score higher, for the tests did not measure the areas in which we had made the greatest strides.

I turned to the National Institute of Mental Health, where I had served as the second-ever black professional on the staff. I tell this story reluctantly, for it will appear to be about bad people. It is not. It is an important story about organizational relationships and networking, and it illustrates the roadblocks encountered by projects addressing minority needs when minorities are not a large enough part of mainstream institutions and when the political tide turns against the poor.

Several years earlier, I had been one of the founders of the Black Psychiatrists of America. As an NIMH staff member, I had observed the way a number of grant proposals by black scholars were passed over because they did not meet the review committee's preference for experimental research design. This design tries to set up constant conditions in a control and an experimental group, and then observe the effect of one modification in the experimental group. For example, with a special curriculum, you contrast the performance of otherwise comparable students using the traditional curriculum and using the special curriculum.

Such experimental research design, however, can never address the multiple and dynamic interactions of complex systems. To the black psychiatrists, I recommended that we ask the NIMH to create a minority center that would use research designs more fitted to work in the real world. Also, having been at the NIMH, I knew where the money was, so I recommended an actual operating center rather than one that simply coordinated research activities.

An important lesson: When the Minority Center was created, using some of the funds from another operating center, a member of the center whose budget was accordingly reduced (and who had regularly presented himself as a friend of blacks) angrily said, "You niggers won't even know what to do with millions of dollars!" Not only was the comment racist, but more important, it betrayed a fear of diminished control of scarce resources and an unwillingness to allow the less powerful to help determine their own destiny—the approach we used in our SDP project. It doesn't help much to call somebody a racist. But we should remember that racism is fundamentally about power and control.

We presented our SDP Social Skills Curriculum for Inner-City Children proposal to a highly qualified multiracial review panel of the Minority Center containing people from backgrounds that allowed them to intuitively understand the potential of our approach—and we received support. This program had grown out of discussions about what the children would need to have a chance to achieve the American Dream. Parents and staff together agreed they would need social and academic skills in politics and government, business and economics, health and nutrition. They would also need skills related to spiritual and leisure-time activities.

Our work suggested that education and mental health organizations ought to be working together. But when I tried to develop a proposal for a center that would allow us to do intervention research supported by both the National Institute of Mental Health and the National Institute of Education, things fell apart completely. We were not known to NIE, and too many of the decision makers didn't understand the need for our approach. Again, we almost lost all program support.

Around the same time, during a trip to St. Louis, I happened to run into Donald Suggs, a dentist who was a school friend and an African American from a background similar to my own. Over a casual breakfast, I described our work. With no training in the behavioral or social sciences, he immediately understood the wisdom of our approach and offered arguments in support of it based on his own life and work experiences. This was not surprising, for what we were and are doing is plain common sense (or perhaps, as a colleague characterized it, *uncommon* common sense).

In connection with a subsequent application, NIMH site visitors from a traditional review panel came to New Haven to get a better sense of what we were trying to do. It was early in the 1980s, and the government was being pressured to get out of social research. (Unfortunately, some of the pressure came from biological researchers because it would mean more resources for them.) Our parents and teachers were bursting with pride about what they had been able to accomplish. By then, the all-important test scores had improved. The panel reviewers acknowledged that these were remarkable inner-city schools.

But sentiment was going against us, and one supportive reviewer, trying to be helpful, asked me to explain again whether the improved social climate was the independent or dependent variable. Several teachers looked at me in utter disbelief: What was this academic-bureaucratic gibberish all about? Another group at the NIMH was about to support us when one member of the panel reminded them that our intervention research did not conform to experimental research design. We didn't get support from them, either.

We had a good proposal, an unmatched track record, good community and university support, potential for national impact, and our work was well known to the NIMH staff and reviewers. Generally, my strategy when facing a blocked door is to keep my cool and search for one that is open. But we desperately needed support, and I wasn't being treated like a member of the club. While discussing the rejection decision with the review section chief, a friend, I blew up. He listened quietly and finally said, "I'm sorry, Jim. I think you understand."

I did. Most of the people at the NIMH wanted to support efforts to address difficult social problems. But the tide of political power was turning against minorities and the poor. This was not professional peer review, it was political action.

In 1992, a congressional committee member who heard my testimony found it incredible that we had not been able to get government support, despite the fact that I was well qualified, from a low-income African American background, with experiences and training that should have been of great interest to people trying to address problems in low-income African American communities.

Perhaps this rejection had nothing to do with either the merits of our proposal or our approach to solving social problems. This concern was expressed by the late Ron Edmonds, and it influenced a major decision that we made. At the time, Ron was on the faculty of the Harvard School of Education and was also working with the New York City school chancellor's office. Ron had detailed the conditions under which schools serving nonmainstream students were successful, and he challenged schools to create them. I was concerned that many schools would attempt to do so without being properly trained. Good ideas might be thrown out because of poor implementation. I felt that more demonstration of successful practices in the field was needed. Ron feared that there was an effort afoot in America to write off low-income and minority students. Some research then gaining attention suggested that schools couldn't make a difference, and Ron predicted it would be used to support this effort.

Meanwhile, at Yale, we were debating whether to seek support to follow our students over time and learn more about how to create very good schools or whether to disseminate what we already knew, which was enough to create reasonably good schools. We decided to try for a nucleus of reasonably good schools in which young people from disadvantaged backgrounds demonstrated that they could perform well.

At that point, serendipity struck twice. Bob Haggerty, then the president of the William T. Grant Foundation, felt that it was important to support some of the programs with successful track records that the federal government would not support. Federal judge Douglas W. Hillman heard about our work and ordered the Benton Harbor, Michigan, school district to implement it as partial settlement in a school segregation case. Between them, they provided an opportunity to field-test the model, although a court order created its own set of problems.

To complicate matters, I made an error by training our first out-of-state facilitator, Erma Mitchell, for a year in New Haven. When she returned to her district, the attitude of her colleagues was "You had a wonderful sabbatical year at Yale; now you change us." The essence of the SDP process is participation and belonging. I had forgotten or not yet fully understood that the three most important parts of successful school change are relationships, relationships, relationships.

Benton Harbor superintendent James Hawkins visited our project schools in New Haven and became convinced that the model could work. He sent a group that was representative of all the adults involved in schools in Benton Harbor for an orientation of several days. This group experience created a bond among key people and a shared understanding. When they returned to Benton Harbor, they could create and sustain the necessary positive relationships. They were then able to make significant social and academic gains.

In several studies, we compared Benton Harbor students in SDP schools to students in non-SDP schools. The studies showed significant student gains in achievement, attendance, behavior, and overall adjustment. But Benton Harbor had serious financial problems and three superintendents in five years. Because conditions in a community affect conditions in a school, it is difficult to maintain improved levels of functioning in schools for very long without reasonable stability in the surrounding community. While some of the SDP principles continue to be used by some staff members, we no longer work with this school system.

Our second district outside Connecticut became a prototype for our later expansion and has become the location of one of our Regional Professional Development Centers. John Murphy, then the new superintendent of the Prince George's County School District in Maryland, contacted me in 1984 about implementing our program. They had little money, so we brought Jan Stocklinski, the SDP facilitator, to New Haven for a month and had the representative group of adults join her in the last few days. They went back and began to implement the model in ten elementary schools. In three years, the ten schools showed twice the rate of academic improvement of the other district schools.

Several other districts followed, but we struggled to survive financially. Generous grants from several foundations still left us far short of what we needed to intervene on a large scale and with far less than what we had received from federal government grants. Then, serendipity struck again. Hugh Price became vice president of the Rockefeller Foundation.

Hugh's father, Kline Price, was a physician and one of my teachers in medical school. Marilyn Price, Hugh's wife, was the daughter of my anatomy teacher there. I got to know them when Hugh attended law school at Yale and Marilyn was a teacher in the New Haven elementary school where I did my first work during my child psychiatry training. Our families occasionally socialized, and we shared an interest in social problems affecting the black community.

After Hugh finished law school, he passed up lucrative opportunities and took a low-paying job as the first director of a grassroots advocacy organization, the New Haven Black Coalition. The Prices lived in a house across the street from one of our SDP schools, and their daughter was a student there. Hugh was in the audience the night we were harshly criticized and the program was almost discontinued. He watched us hang on, turn things around, and help create a good school.

He went on to gain experiences in urban development with a private firm; in hands-on city management on the staff of Mayor Frank Logue in New Haven; as editorial writer for the *New York Times*; as vice president of WNET-TV, the New York City public television station; and then, important to our work, as vice president of the Rockefeller Foundation, responsible for the $5 million annual education portfolio. He is now president of the National Urban League.

The Rockefeller Foundation, in 1990, was looking for a way to make a significant contribution to a public education universe where about $230 billion is spent annually on some 80,000 kindergarten-through-twelfth-grade schools, approximately 15,000 of which serve disadvantaged students. The foundation sought a project that addressed what they called the gaps in the school reform movement that were identified by Secretary of Education Terrel Bell in his 1983 report *A Nation at Risk* (National Commission on Excellence in Education, 1983).

The major gaps were the developmental and school climate issues. Most current reforms focused on curriculum, instruction, assessment, and using technology. The Rockefeller Foundation strategy, like ours, was to disseminate a model that was a work in progress but not "the answer." The idea was to get a significant number of schools *to put the child first* and work entirely from this idea.

Hugh believed that our project meshed with their interests. But because of our long-standing friendship, he consulted with many people across the country besides me. The work of the SDP was widely known by now through a 1988 *Scientific American* article I had written and through many other articles and presentations over the years, and our project was repeatedly cited by the consultants as one that best met the Rockefeller Foundation's criteria.

The Rockefeller Foundation provided the first solid support we had had in ten years and brought renewed attention to our ideas. It has enabled us to move to a model in which district-based leadership teams learn the SDP process and, in turn, help local school districts use it.

We see here between Hugh Price and myself a rare example of an African American old-school friendship-based mainstream network in action. But what we really need is a larger African American network because our common experiences create essential understanding and skills, and a greater sense of urgency. The lack of such a network sometimes leads to unintended exclusion from mainstream economic participation and benefits.

The School Development Program Today

Our present organization and work are still based on our pre-Rockefeller experiences and on what we have learned as we have worked with more and more schools. Our initial strategy was to get the SDP used in a nucleus of schools that was large enough to trigger replication in many places. This is a widely accepted computer-parallel view of school reform—click, copy, move cursor, and paste. Another popular notion is that successful models will stimulate competition and the elimination of bad educational practice. On reflection, our experiences suggest that this is not the most useful way to think about large-scale school improvement.

We began expansion efforts at a nearby school in New Haven in the 1970s. The principal told me that we would not have the same success at his school as we did at our initial school, King Elementary, since that school served children from single-family homes, while his school served children from project apartments. I noted that our other school, Brennan Elementary, had improved despite the fact that its children were from project buildings, at that time with an open garbage dump nearby. He countered that those were two-story dwellings and his school served high-rise project buildings. What he was saying was "These children can't learn."

To his credit, he did facilitate the process and help to improve the social and academic performance of the students. On one occasion, he described a staff breakfast, prepared by the male teachers for the female teachers as part of the plan to improve school climate. He glowed as he spoke. Then, as a puzzled afterthought, he said, "You know, it was odd. There wasn't a single discipline problem that day."

The fact is that intangibles like climate do affect behavior and performance. But many well-meaning people just don't get it. And even when they do, the skills and the courage to change can be a problem. Sometimes the teachers' employers and the community send conflicting signals—change by doing more of the same. Confused, with little support, some school staff respond to pressure for improvement with the attitude that "This too will pass." Some leaders get involved in change programs for the wrong reasons—to look progressive or to change enough to deflect criticism. In one case, a chaotic school was brought under control with a child development approach. With a school the principal now enjoyed and thought he could control, he went back to the old way of doing things, and the school collapsed.

Another school district in Connecticut asked our YCSC team to intervene without designating a local person responsible for internal change. We explained why this was not likely to work, but because of their insistence and because we could learn from the experience, we agreed to do so. As expected, it didn't work. It was too easy for those who didn't want change to turn others against outsiders. We were not there for the informal exchanges and interactions that can clarify confusion and promote trust. Most important, the interest in improvement must come from a significant group of school, central office, and board leaders, and it must grow as the process is implemented. The effort must be tailored to local conditions—personnel, political, social, and economic—all of which involve hot-button issues that an outsider cannot easily grasp.

These are some of the reasons that the notion of exact replication is not very useful in thinking about creating a world-class education system nationwide. Our challenge has been to encourage schools and districts to use child development principles to improve practice through the application of the nine elements of our SDP model. Very early, it became apparent that we could not expect *exact* replication. But it appeared possible for school groups to gain deep understanding, build good organizations, and apply program principles in a way that is tailored to a particular setting.

Our small New Haven–based staff could not manage to take us from 66 schools in 1988 to more than 650 schools in 1997. This growth was made possible through our partnerships with several schools of education, several state departments of education, and one mental health organization, Youth Guidance, in Chicago, which worked with us *and* with local school districts. We have also developed a national faculty, most of whom learned to implement the SDP through the partnerships and are now an important resource pool for us.

We sought partners who could benefit from working with local school districts and would provide our program with a chance to learn about agencies that are obvious candidates for collaboration on future large-scale state and federal government school change efforts.

In our SDP book *Rallying the Whole Village,* Deborah Smith and Louise Kaltenbaugh (1996) describe the partnership among Southern University at New Orleans, the SDP, and the New Orleans public schools. The School of Education reformed its teacher preparation program by requiring that its pre-service teachers do fieldwork in SDP schools as an integral part of their professional courses beginning in their *sophomore* year. Smith and Kaltenbaugh teamed up with Jennifer Patterson, the SDP facilitator, and Mary Thompson of the district's central office to form an educational change team. In 1993–94, a cadre of 288 university students were involved in the K–16 Partnership, working as mathematics tutors, reading assistants, speech and hearing diagnosticians, health and nutrition assistants, art enrichment assistants, and social work interns in the SDP schools.

In another example, the partnership consists of the Cleveland public schools, Cleveland State University, the Cleveland Child Guidance Center, and the Harvard Business School Club of Cleveland, whose members associate themselves with SDP schools and work with businesses surrounding the schools to foster their support (Haynes, Emmons, Gebreyesus, and Ben-Avie, 1996).

Our partners gain SDP skills before and after implementation in their home districts by attending our two-week training programs in New Haven along with leaders from the local districts with whom they are collaborating. Our staff helps them gain the knowledge and skill needed to coach district-based implementation teams. There is a weeklong leadership academy for principals, and scheduled site visits and periodic communication between our staff and local leadership. While the training, called the Comer Project for Change in Education (CPCE) and directed by Edward Joyner, has become much more sophisticated, the focus on child development and learning through implementation of the basic nine elements of the program has not changed.

Numerous schools are using the SDP on the initiative of local people who have not received training. Interestingly enough, some of these schools have made excellent social and academic gains. Unfortunately, some show little improvement, even with training.

Some have said that our approach is helpful only for low-income, minority-group children. Until recently, districts that had significant social problems and poor test scores—often in minority communities—were the most interested. But others have recognized that the SDP's mechanisms and ways of working can be helpful in preparing all young people to function well in a more complex time when more support for development is needed and less is available. Actually, the practices we have developed are closer to those in elite private schools than in most public schools.

The SDP is operating in school districts serving diverse ethnic, cultural, and socioeconomic communities. Valencia Park Elementary School in San Diego, California, serves twenty-five different linguistic groups in an affluent area. In Seattle, View Ridge Elementary School serves a mixture of African American, Asian, and white students in an upper middle-class residential neighborhood. In Meriden, Connecticut, the Pulaski Elementary School's student population is predominantly white. In Guilford County, North Carolina, SDP schools are in large and small cities, rural areas, and towns, and the students are black and white (Haynes, Gebreyesus, and Comer, 1993).

Outcomes and Implications

In sum, our experience shows that with the SDP, schools can be improved. And we have demonstrated that a faithful application of the nine basic components, in which necessary organization and child development principles are embedded, will produce good outcomes without cookie-cutter conformity. I could relate innumerable anecdotes and other indicators of success, some almost embarrassing.

One principal told me that the program probably saved her life. When she saw I thought that was hyperbole, she said, "No, literally." She explained that she had had a heart attack as a new principal trying to jam change down the throat of a resistant school community.

But when she subsequently used the SDP model to share power, she helped to bring about significant social and academic improvement and greatly reduced her own stress level.

A previously failing school serving a housing project won first place in the *Scholastic Magazine* mathematics scavenger hunt contest for two years in a row, in competition with more than a thousand schools across the country—many middle-income, some elite and private. And schools in California, Florida, Maryland, North Carolina, and elsewhere have won state and national awards for excellence.

I recently attended the third anniversary of ten SDP schools in Detroit. When we initiated the project in the same auditorium, I saw doubt and apprehension on the faces of parents and staff. This time, the enthusiasm when each participating school was announced rivaled that shown for the Detroit Pistons. I have experienced similar enthusiasm at such events in Prince George's County, Maryland; in Chicago; in San Francisco; and elsewhere. And many students in these schools are making significant social and academic gains.

Many parents have been motivated to improve their own education, employment, and lives through their involvement in our improvement process. A long-distance telephone operator recognized me as the caller and introduced herself as a former King School parent. She intimated that before her work at the school, she did not have the confidence to take and hold such a job. Several parents from my time of direct involvement who were once in perilous life situations have returned to school and are now successful social workers, teachers, and, in one case, a state agency executive.

Students from these low-income but no longer low-quality academic settings have earned degrees at highly competitive colleges. Some are now educators, physicians, engineers, and businesspeople. Numerous teachers and principals around the country who have been able to make the process work in their schools are now in leadership positions in their districts. Students and staff report (and reflect) better relations and motivation in middle-income areas as well.

Because policies and practices are established locally, statistical data on social and academic achievement vary in availability and comparability. Nonetheless, our director of research, Norris Haynes, has shown that students who attended SDP schools had significantly higher scores on self-concept, social competence, resilience, attendance, and academic achievement. And in less quantifiable areas, our case studies show families becoming active partners with school staff, and teachers expressing more positive perceptions of their students and collaborating more with each other following SDP implementation (Haynes, 1994). Our best approximation suggests that after three years, about a third of the schools make significant social and academic improvement, a third show a modest improvement which is often difficult to sustain, and a third show no gain. Assessments by evaluators outside our program support our guesstimate. The success of remarkable school leaders and their staffs, working alone or with our own and other national reform projects, and the approach used in elite schools show common threads: *positive school relationships; caring, responsible, predictable adults in the lives of students; a sense of belonging in constructive groups engaged in challenging learning and activities; and opportunity for students to sense direction and purpose.*

In short, many people know what it takes to improve schools. On the other hand, school improvement takes a long time and affects too few. We expected achievement of certain goals in our initial project schools by 1973, but didn't reach that level until 1984. We did not expect our ideas to be readily accepted, but we also did not anticipate the multiple and complex problems we encountered in and beyond the schools.

Also, we know that if families and communities are functioning poorly, children cannot come to school ready to learn. We know that if teachers are not carefully selected, prepared, and supported, we cannot create a world-class school system. We know that education is critical to the future of our economy and democracy. Given what we know about schooling, its importance, and the fact that almost everybody would like to improve it, why are we not making the adjustments needed?

All of this caused me to look beyond the overt and acknowledged reasons for school problems and to take a close look at our founding myths, how they are invoked, and how they have limited the effectiveness of many community, family, and school policies and practices. I explore the two most troublesome—intelligence and motivation, and African Americans as losers—elsewhere.

It is natural to want to hold on to the meaningful old ways of doing things, no matter how limiting—and once aware of the need for change, to try to go forth and improve opportunities for all without addressing the past. But we can't do either. The painful work of discovering and understanding the effects of the past on all of us is needed to end our paralysis and to enable us to create policies and programs that help us achieve the Good Society (my Good Society, fueled by LBJ's Great Society) that is our goal.

References

Cohen, D. J., and Solnit, A. J. "Foreword." In J. P. Comer, N. M. Haynes, E. T. Joyner, and Ben-Avie, M. eds., *Rallying the Whole Village: The Comer Process for Reforming Education.* New York: Teachers College Press, 1996, pp. xi–xvi.

Comer, J. P. "Educating Poor Minority Children." *Scientific American,* November 1988, 256, 42–48.

Haynes, N. M., ed. *School Development Program Research Monograph.* New Haven, Conn.: Yale Child Study Center, 1994.

Haynes, N. M., Emmons, C. L., Gebreyesus, S., and Ben-Avie, M. "The School Development Program Evaluation Process." In J. P. Comer, N. M. Haynes, E. T. Joyner, and

M. Ben-Avie, eds., *Rallying the Whole Village: The Comer Process for Reforming Education.* New York: Teachers College Press, 1996, 123–146.

Haynes, N. M., Gebreyesus, S., and Comer, J. P. *Selected Case Studies of National Implementation of the School Development Program.* New Haven, Conn.: Yale Child Study Center, 1993.

National Commission on Excellence in Education. *A Nation at Risk: The Imperative for Educational Reform: A Report to the Nation and the Secretary of Education, United States Department of Education.* Washington D.C.: National Commission on Excellence in Education, 1983.

Smith, D. B., and Kaltenbaugh, L.P.S. "University-School Partnership: Reforming Teacher Preparation." In J. P. Comer, N. M. Haynes, E. T. Joyner, and M. Ben-Avie, eds., *Rallying the Whole Village: The Comer Process for Reforming Education.* New York: Teachers College Press, 1996, 42–71.

6

To Leave No Child Behind

Why, what, and how we learned about schools over thirty-five years of work is presented in the 2004 book *Leave No Child Behind*. What we've learned corroborates our original notion that constructive interactions between children and youth, their caretakers, and the authority figures in their lives support their development, learning, and performance as well as their preparation for adult life. But traditional goals and approaches to teaching that all but ignore relationship and developmental issues have created resistance in everybody who belongs to what I call the *education enterprise*—some teachers and parents, schools of education, and policymakers at every level—to the changes in all areas of schooling that could address staff and student needs. This chapter discusses the ways in which we changed the focus of our collaboration from school to central office and beyond to try to overcome entrenched resistance. It suggests that deep systemic change—in order to leave no child behind—can be brought about through a focus on preparation of the current and future workforce, enabling the workforce to create school cultures that can support parent, staff, and community collaboration in intentional support of student development and learning.

WHEN I WAS A YOUNG PSYCHIATRIST, I WOULD STOP BY HOME when I had a trip in the Chicago area. My mother was always a little uncertain about "this psychiatry business." She had sacrificed so that I could become a "real doctor." She wanted to know what I was doing in schools. As I explained, she listened, and listened, and listened for more, and finally said, "Is that all? It sounds a lot like common sense to me." She thought a moment more and said, "And they pay you for that?!!"

My mother had less than two years of formal education, but she understood that children behave and perform best when their caretakers provide them with good preparatory experiences. She felt that everybody must know that. Our work has focused on providing such support in schools. I recently described our SDP framework to the president of a prestigious university. His response: "It's so obvious. Why is it not being done?"

It is common sense and an obvious need. There is an enormous body of scientific literature, now buttressed by brain research, that suggests that child and youth development should be the foundation for academic learning. Throughout *Leave No Child Behind*, I discuss how such knowledge can be applied to improve schools, by those serving the most marginalized students as well as those serving the most privileged. The price of not using low-cost opportunities to prevent the high-cost problems that result from not adequately supporting child and youth development should interest policymakers and taxpayers alike. But the inertia and resistance to doing what is needed is great.

In another chapter of *Leave No Child Behind*, I described the inertia and resistance our SDP team encountered at the individual school level, largely because of tradition and fear of change. We eventually realized that the same is true in other *secondary* or service networks and in the *tertiary* or policy networks, as well as in the *primary* family networks. Behaviors that influence education outcomes take place in all three. Keeping things the way they are is a widespread way of trying to deal with the threat of the unknown involved in change. This tendency creates more problems than it solves or prevents in this age of rapid change.

The political, economic, and social forces operating to maintain the status quo are even more powerful than the psychological forces. It often takes courage to protect the little ones or to provide opportunity for the less powerful. A superintendent told me that he just had to bite the bullet and fire two teacher assistants who were repeatedly abusive of children, even though one was a relative and the other a close friend of one of his board members, who was pushing for their retention. In the 1930s, a white school board member and his family in Mississippi left town under the threat of death because he suggested that the disparity between funds for the white schools and the black be dropped from 90 percent to 80 percent.

And which computers should we buy, anyway? There are a multitude of purchasing and employment decisions that can be affected by changes in school and district leadership, programs, and ways of working. In most places, there is no fire wall between the delivery of education services and local politics. The needs and changes in local political leadership impact education policy, for better and for worse. Bureaucracy is often cited as a huge problem, and it is a major source of inertia. But it is the way people function and relate that makes it a problem.

Unfortunately, even when poor and marginalized people get a voice, their knowledge base often limits their ability to do what is in the best interest of their children. In our early pilot project years, and until a collaborative and success-oriented culture emerged, members of our Yale team sometimes found themselves tactfully protecting the best interest of the children in opposition to the demands of parent leaders—such as using project money to hire full-time doctors and nurses. Given the lack of clarity about the mission of schools and how to measure success, this is often true of affluent, well-educated people as well. Making decisions about how to improve complex systems like schools is a challenging process for all.

While there are many kinds and sources of inertia, there are two that carry unmatched power. They are the platform on which many other difficult issues stand and grow. The first is the inequitable way that we fund our education system—particularly property taxes and the failure to make adjustments for low-tax base, high-need areas. The second is our focus on curriculum, instruction, and testing or assessment without providing adequate support for development.

Both produce outcomes that make it possible to use very powerful myths and rationalizations to obfuscate the real causes of underachievement and problem behaviors. Indeed, the resistance to a developmental perspective is rooted in the most powerful and widespread of many myths—that school learning is a product of genetically determined intelligence and will only. Thus, "They are not able, are not responsible, are not interested, will take our jobs," and more. Usually left unsaid is a belief that it is not cost-effective to invest more in the education of poor and marginalized students. Reactions to these myths lead to conflict and struggle rather than problem solving.

For these and for many other reasons that benefit various groups of mainstream adults, school improvement approaches that would obviously help all students are not taken, even when the approaches are supported by research-based evidence. In order to effectively push for change, we must greatly weaken these rationalizations and myths. From the beginning of our SDP work, we have felt that helping to achieve success where it is not expected is the best way to weaken resistance and to promote support for large-scale school improvement for all students. I have not forgotten that the town of Westbury voted against a school bond issue even after the district made extraordinary gains, but continued and more widespread school success among students from difficult backgrounds cannot be ignored indefinitely.

To speed up the process, the dots must be connected for parents, community leaders, and others—for example, by focusing on the high cost of inadequate education when known ways to improve it exist. Also, we have not done enough to call attention to public school successes and how the numbers can be increased by addressing student underdevelopment and staff underpreparation. More must be done to point out the danger of not preparing students from all backgrounds and of all achievement levels to promote and protect our democratic way of life. Providing evidence (existing successful schools and districts) and exposing the many myths and rationalizations should begin to help many more people see their own best interest in the improved education and adult functioning of all children, to enable many more to understand, as did the building principals in our pilot schools, that by thinking and working differently, we can create a win-win situation.

To leave no child behind, we need a *change strategy* in which we use proven knowledge and skills that reduce inertia and resistance in schools and districts, that will create a present and future educator workforce capable of using proven approaches, and that will help decision makers in all networks create policies that will enable education practitioners to create school programs that will support good student development, instruction, and learning. Although this is a daunting task, it is possible because, just as we found in our pilot schools in 1968, today most people—not all—want good public schools.

When it becomes apparent that such schools can be created regularly, at lower short- and long-term costs than inadequate schooling, it will be possible to mobilize the level of political pressure needed to strongly promote improved education as social justice, the bedrock of American democracy. The appeal to our essence as a nation—and making the economic benefits apparent—will override existing inertia and resistance. This is the way American democracy has worked, from the soldiers who fought in the War of the Revolution, wrestling reasonable opportunities from the landed aristocracy, to the modern civil rights and women's movements.

The political pressure is growing, and it will increase as parents, educators, and employers call for real solutions. But traditional curriculum-, instruction-, and assessment-oriented approaches, even with recent reforms, will not be enough. Until we adequately focus on the underlying problem of underdevelopment and the under-preparation of caretakers at home and at school, we will not have a viable alternative ready when a strong commitment to good public school education is made. My concern is that we will be like a friend of mine who participated in the North Carolina drugstore sit-ins against racial segregation. When they finally agreed to serve him, he did not have a dime for a cup of coffee.

A brief review of the changes and the challenges in the nature of community and society and the lack of change in the needs of children and youth for support of their development helps to make the resistance a bit more understandable, and suggests the kind of understanding that is needed among practitioners and policymakers.

The support for development once naturally embedded in less complex communities and the safety valve of earning a living without a good education have been greatly diminished. None of our institutions have created systems of support that will adequately meet this basic and irrepressible need of the young.

Our Yale Child Study Center team approached these challenges by asking what it is that children and youth are "brain wired" to do and what conditions will lead to constructive outcomes. In *Leave No Child Behind,* I pointed out that children are born exploring their environment in the service of survival. While learning is rooted in this powerful, basic human need and impulse, academic learning is not. Academic learning can, however, become an important tool for survival, for successfully addressing life's tasks, and for finding meaning and purpose in life. This occurs best when caretakers and institutions respect and facilitate the child's need and impulse to grow or develop along all the pathways that contribute to successful functioning in the world—physical, social-interactive, psychological-emotional, ethical, linguistic, and cognitive-intellectual.

Our education system focuses first on instruction, with or without adequate development. I have heard school people say they wished that the students were as enthusiastic about their studies as they are about their time with their friends, their fads, their appearances, and more. That enthusiasm stems from the fact that they are engaged in growth activities that are the essence of being human. They are in the process of growing up and away from dependency and vulnerability. And just as most, with the help of caretakers, begin to manage their bodies and their environment reasonably well, their bodies and often their environment begin to change rapidly, and they need to modify their relationship with their families to continue to grow. Making it in the world is more clearly becoming their responsibility. These are anxiety-provoking, threatening situations.

As they use their not-yet-well-socialized-or-channeled aggressive or survival energy to deal with all of this, a great deal of confusion, uncertainty, noise, anger and sometimes fights, frustration, disappointment, and the like take place. This is often mixed with joy, exuberance, a desire to challenge and to be challenged. All of this is grist for the academic learning mill, but we treat it as a bother. By doing so, we forfeit our opportunity to establish pupil-staff-parent relationships that will enable school people and parents to become meaningful in positive ways because we help them *grow and learn* rather than force them to *learn without adequate growth*. When school staffs understand the struggle to grow that is going on with students—and the power and potential this represents—they can tap into this ferment to make academic learning meaningful and exciting (Sizer, 1996).

This was the focus of the Social Skills Curriculum for Inner-City Children. The prime developmental impulse of elementary school–age children is to work and achieve things, to be like adults around them. The content and methods of this project were consistent with adult life participation, including the consideration and practice of appropriate behaviors, self and situation management skills, rights, responsibilities, and much more. The staff, the parents, and the students together provided the engine that pulled the curriculum, instruction, and learning. This approach often brought the community into the school and took the school into the community; it engaged all in the support of growth along important developmental pathways. In traditional schools, curriculum and instruction are expected to pull the students along.

As important as academic learning is, it must be remembered that it is a tool and an aspect of development. It is important to remember that development is the primary need and the precursor, when not the prerequisite for academic learning. In the case of many children who have inadequate preparatory experiences, academic instruction is like trying to hang out clothes to dry without a clothesline or clothespins. A teacher friend added "on a windy day" to this analogy. There is too little overall development to utilize the information being poured in; perhaps "lay on" makes the point better here. The healthy child will turn away, withdraw, or act out rather than fail. The emotional attachment to parents and teachers provide the "line" and the "clothespins."

Throughout this book, I have mentioned good education practice in highly successful schools serving marginalized students who were not expected to achieve at a high level. Recall that student academic success often followed staff helping them manage relationship and performance challenges. And academic, relationship, and behavior problems were often prevented by adequately preparing students to manage challenges in their environment before engaging in activities that would promote excessive threat. Students are most open to help with their growth when there is a reasonable degree of continuity of relationships with key and caring caretakers. They need reasonably safe places where they can express themselves, where they can engage in activities that help them begin to figure out who they are, what skills they have, where they want to go, what it takes on their part to get there, how to begin to take responsibility for themselves, and, generally, what it takes to be a good human being, liked and respected by others. The school, like the home, is a venue in which young people attend to their primary challenge—developing in these ways and growing up and away from dependency and vulnerability.

I want to make this point again and finally: students who are developing well will learn well. I acknowledge differences in aptitude, potential, talents, traits, and more. But the task of public and private education systems is to promote optimal growth and preparation for adult life among all. This requires adequate support for development of all.

The case I have made here suggests that all teachers, administrators, and professional support staff should be prepared, in both pre-service and in-service; to create a school context, community, or culture that enables them to explore student development and use it to make academic work meaningful and useful to students in promoting their own full development. The obvious implication here is that schools of education must prepare their students to help support development at several levels and points of influence in and out of school. The less obvious implication is the need to change a deep-seated education culture obstacle.

Education reformers often look to medicine and law for models that will guide improvement in their own professional practice.

Because making a diagnosis is often difficult, and there is variance in the response to treatment, a culture of consultation emerged in medicine. As a physician and an outsider, I have always been struck by the absence of a culture of consultation in education. In most schools, there is no time built in for colleagues to plan, to reflect on their practice and its outcomes with each other, to share insights and understandings. Indeed, the individual teacher is supposed to have a knowledge base that is applicable to all students, all the time. But students are not inanimate objects. Each is different in the way they think, learn, and behave.

Actually, teaching is more like psychotherapy. The relationship with the teacher, like that with the therapist, is a part of the "treatment." The cause of "disease" often stems from dysfunctions that are more amorphous than those in the more biology-based medicine, the treatments are less definitive, and the outcomes are less easily observed and measured than with largely biology-based problems. Trying to understand the challenge facing a student and how to address it is at least as difficult as making a diagnosis in medicine. Good teaching, like good child rearing, requires an ongoing action research approach, with professional colleagues sharing and learning how to best meet student needs.

Indeed, this is the best model for student learning. Shared thinking; problem assessment; thinking about how children think; thinking about how to help them think about the way *they* think, how to use thought to explore the world around them; and more leads to deep understanding and an interest in thinking as a tool for academic learning and for general learning and expression. A school staff working in this way provides a useful model for student thinking and growth. Teachers, for the most part, are isolated practitioners. When teachers are able to work together and examine their practice, something all professionals should do, they experience mutual support and less stress.

Many schools of education do not prepare students to work in this way. A veteran teacher who recently participated in our SDP 102 training session, a year after she attended 101, asked, "Where is Dr. Comer? I don't even know the man, but I want to give him a big hug! This is what we should have learned in college!" She did, and she's right. *All the money we spend on research, training, equipment, instructional programs, and the like will give us too small a return on our investment until we help the adults working together in a building learn to create a culture in which they can collaborate with each other in a way that will support the development of students.*

For students, their family life, kin, network of friends, organizations to which they feel a sense of belonging, and community-based health, recreation, housing, and other services impact their ability to develop and learn just as much as, if not more than what they learn in the classroom. The effects of these experiences outside the classroom are cumulative, as are what happens in school. In other chapters in *Leave No Child Behind,* I pointed out that we spend a significant amount on support services but that we are not getting the bang for the buck that we should from these services because they are fragmented, do not promote a continuity of relationships, and, very important, particularly in health, housing, and welfare services, are often impersonal and demeaning rather than supportive of good family functioning and child and youth development.

It is not possible to save every child or to fix every ill in the world. People must help themselves and not count on government or philanthropy to do so. And most people want to help themselves to the extent possible. Our sense of adequacy depends on it. The problem is that services that were once available from emotionally meaningful people in most primary social networks now reside in the more impersonal secondary social networks of schools, workplaces, health care provider locations, and other places. Too often, there are barriers between those in need of service and the providers. Not enough attention has been given to how people can access these services in ways that are not demeaning.

For many, simply needing help is demeaning, and the status, attitude, and behavior of the helper is often perceived as a part of the problem until the helper-client interaction proves otherwise. Powerful issues, such as positive identity, self-respect, self-confidence, fear of failure, a sense of adequacy, trust, and much more, are at play when a human being, groups, or nations seek to help one another, particularly when social marginalization, past dominance, or exclusion has been a factor. It is human nature.

What does the two-year-old say? "I'll do it myself." Affected by the same concerns, leaders in third-world or underdeveloped countries have sometimes wanted to place outside helpers in their best-functioning communities rather than in those with the greatest need. A black student was performing at a very low level on a test given by a white psychologist until they took a break. During the break, he observed his tester's black colleague warmly embrace her, and his performance improved dramatically when the testing resumed. A black physician working to help dysfunctional families was challenged by one participant, who said, "What right do you have to tell me how to live?" Many years ago, the three Comer brothers, all college students, tried to encourage a relative still in high school who had demonstrated outstanding academic ability but had no family support and was drifting toward trouble. While he didn't say what was said to the doctor, on reflection, his nonverbal behavior and demeanor conveyed the same message.

But a continued lack of success on the part of the two-year-old— and anybody else—can lead to defeat, hopelessness, dependency, and worse. Because many young people will not have a chance to experience reasonable success without adequate supportive relationships and services, we must give great attention to how we can provide them in an empowering way.

What enables the two-year-old to accept help when the task is too great? It is a relationship in which the caretaker demonstrates genuine respect and commitment to full growth and opportunity for the child. A similar relationship is needed when working with underdeveloped or marginalized individuals or groups of all ages. Help must be provided—beginning in the home, continued through school, into the community and the larger society—in a way that promotes a level of self-respect and confidence that can lead to successful independent and responsible interdependent mainstream functioning.

The school can collaborate with community services to provide continual, integrated, personalized support for development in a way that no other service provider standing alone really can. It is the social organization best positioned to link home and community in a reasonably harmonious fashion and simultaneously serve its own interest—help students develop and learn in a way that serves individual interests and protects democracy. When the school can "connect," the school is family. I recall a youngster who ran away after an incident with his mother and was found by his teacher in the cold, in the dark, huddled against his closed schoolhouse door—his other emotionally important "family."

There is a slow but growing understanding that many families and students will need services from meaningful people to be ready and able to perform adequately in school. An example of the kind of relationship that is helpful is provided by Joy Dryfoos (1998), who described a school-based health clinic founded by Aaron Shirley, a local physician and civil rights activist in Jackson, Mississippi, in her book *Full-Service Schools:* "Aaron Shirley and his staff knew the name of every baby in the child-care center. They demonstrated a strong commitment to pregnancy prevention with individual follow-up of every sexually active student who obtained contraceptives from the school clinic."

This school health clinic is a good example of the way services once based in communities and with no relation to schools can be integrated or fused with the work of the schools in support of the overall development of children. The positive attitude and disposition of the providers makes the services respectful and therefore potentially growth-producing. The services—whether health, the arts, athletics, job preparation, preparation for participation in government, indeed, for all aspects of life—can be integrated into the curriculum and instruction activities of schools. The service providers are also additional teaching resources. In short, the essential elements of community that existed in a natural way before the effects of the application of science and technology to all aspects of life can be systematically restored through well-integrated community-based programs in schools.

Our Social Skills Curriculum in the 1970s and 1980s demonstrated that this approach can enliven schools and improve performance among parents, schools, and students across race, income, education, and other differences that could be barriers. Schools working with community services, with supportive dispositions, can promote behaviors and skills needed for mainstream participation needed to prepare young people to protect and promote democracy as adults. The ill effects of marginalization reflected in the troublesome behaviors I described earlier can be reduced.

Some municipalities are trying to put in place similar relationship-sensitive, yet powerful supports and services. Mayors in particular, but also other community leaders, recognize that they must try to bring together human services in a way that will promote inclusion, that will support desirable family functioning and a quality of child rearing that prepares children to elicit the support they need for school success and responsible adult functioning, rather than continue marginality. The challenge is to find a positive way to seamlessly integrate the available inside and outside resources to help school and other service provider staffs overcome negative outside-of-school effects when necessary, to help all students develop adequately.

The mayors are on the front line. The high cost of poor education hurts them first and most. I suspect they are going to be the greatest force for realistic problem solving; that is the way it is supposed to work in a democracy. An initiative undertaken in 2001 by the Institute of Youth, Education, and Families of the National League of Cities (NLC), supported by a grant from the Carnegie Corporation of New York, is a model of the kind of structures and relationships that can be useful. The NLC, the forty-nine state municipal leagues it works with, and the elected leaders of the 1,700 member cities and 18,000 state league cities have the potential of getting the nation to focus on how family and child functioning can shape our national future.

Five cities received a Municipal Leadership in Education grant to bring together community leaders to find ways to work toward providing quality public education. New Haven, Connecticut, was one of the cities selected, along with Charleston, South Carolina; Fort Lauderdale, Florida; Lansing, Michigan; and Portland, Oregon. I serve on the New Haven committee. The committee is co-chaired by Eleanor Osborne, the assistant superintendent of schools for curriculum/instruction, and Sheila Allen Bell, community services administrator for the city of New Haven.

The mayor, John DeStefano, Jr., who gave us the charge, has retained a keen interest in this project. He has since become the president of the National League of Cities. When I first met him a decade ago, he talked about the need to provide better child care, early childhood development, and youth development programs as a way to improve education and to prevent problem behaviors. I was impressed because there were not many public officials who had made that connection, and if they had, they were not talking about it.

About twenty-five people serve on the New Haven committee. They represent almost every segment of the community: parents, teachers union, faith community, business, community college, teachers college, alderman, police, public library, and others. After reviewing the school district's mission and current effort and the resources in the community, we agreed that there was a need to find a way to integrate community services and resources with the school program in a way that would make the help available in a coordinated, emotionally meaningful, and seamless way, and make it continually available, where possible. Otherwise, the start-and-stop help and helpers can be a part of the problem.

This project dovetailed nicely with the New Haven school district's Accountability Plan. Dr. Reginald Mayo, the superintendent, and I had co-chaired the committee that developed the plan over a two-year period. One of our conclusions was that everybody is responsible for the education of a community's children, and we recommended activities and goals for in-school and out-of-school groups. We also asked for measures of success that included, but went beyond test scores. *We hope to measure behaviors and performances that are more directly related to school and adult success, to encourage instructional activities that are true precursors of life success.*

The New York City Department of Education, Office of Youth Development and School-Community Services, headed by senior executive Lester Young, Jr., put together a project entitled Youth Placed at Promise Network. The initiative is in collaboration with the Harlem's Children Zone, Bedford-Stuyvesant Restoration Corporation (BSRC), and the Partnership for After School Education.

Importantly, BSRC, well known for its housing and physical community development over the past thirty years, has made a commitment to people development as the way to revitalize communities. While attention must be given to both, as a nation, we have had a bricks-and-mortar mentality. *The higher level of development needed today requires that we also acquire a people development mentality, that we put in place an infrastructure that makes good child and youth development and learning possible on a large scale.* What is most promising about this project is that dedicated, highly skilled people deeply embedded in the life of the communities involved want to make it happen. The schools and the community-based organizations will have a positive relationship status with non-mainstream families, which should enable them to address sensitive child-rearing issues related to child development and academic learning.

The target communities are Central Harlem in Manhattan and Bedford-Stuyvesant in Brooklyn, communities where 75 and 66 percent of the children, respectively, are born into poverty or marginalized conditions relative to the political, economic, and social mainstream. With children in school at the center of the design, appropriate academic, social, human, and medical services are to be delivered in a way that promotes improved student development, learning, and preparation for successful adult life. The School Development Program framework will help guide the thinking, structuring, and processes involved in implementing this work. An effort will be made, through training and field supports, to promote good developmental practices through seamless home-, school-, and community-based organizations and agency activities. Federal, state, and local government and foundation, public and private financial support is now involved, and collaboration with other community organizations will be sought as the project evolves. The goal is to give these young people an opportunity to experience the American dream like most other Americans.

These fragile efforts are being launched in a swirling, changing tide of political, economic, and social issues. Similar projects that attempted to promote improved social environments have come and gone. And these may not get off the ground. The effort to focus very directly on child and adult development in these projects probably makes them even more vulnerable. Critics call such efforts "soft and fuzzy" and charge that the effects cannot be measured; and some question whether people development is a proper role of government or the appropriate use of taxpayer money.

The critics have a linear and sequential causality conceptual mind-set that does not adequately take the interactivity of individuals with their environments or the interactivity of institutions in the environment into account and does not take feelings and emotions and their relation to development and performance into account. As to the proper role of government, Adam Smith (1904), widely considered the founder of modern economics, suggested three: first, to protect from outside military attack; second, protecting every member of the society from the injustice or oppression of every other member; third, erecting and maintaining public works and institutions that are advantageous to a great society but are not profitable to any individual or small number of individuals.

The third is relevant here. A high level of people development and education, particularly of the low-income working class and poor, is not profitable when done fairly and appropriately, and a great society cannot exist without these conditions. On the other hand, the concerns expressed about such interventions are not without some merit. Social interventions often proceed without a clear theory of change, without appropriate assessment efforts, without mechanisms for change or methods to sustain desirable outcomes. This is what contributes to a fuzzy, directionless, start-and-stop sense about many such programs.

Several programs, past and present, suggest ways, with important changes, that we can simultaneously overcome resistance and provide all students with the kind of support and education that will enable them to be successful adults and to protect our democracy, even in an increasingly complex age. The situation we are in today is similar to that at the turn of the twentieth century, when the nation was moving from an agricultural to an industrial economy. Farmers were working in traditional ways when far more productive techniques were known. Research and demonstration programs at universities and other organizations had better outcomes and were organized in ways to study and do research that would provide knowledge that would bring still better outcomes. But there was no way to bring knowledge to practice, and there was resistance to change.

To overcome the obstacles to improved farming, the Agricultural Extension Service evolved from several existing programs. The service systematically brought improved methods to farmers, informed resisters of the benefits in working differently, and provided financial incentives, and its success overcame the remaining inertia and resistance. It also made America the breadbasket of the world. This helped the country take a lead in industrial development and, eventually, in science and technology. Good education for all is the key to continued American economic leadership and support for democracy in the world. An Education Extension Service (EES) could address the obstacles to improving education at this early stage of the twenty-first century.

An Education Extension Service—with development, learning, and preparation of students for adult life as a central focus—could provide the kind of framework and infrastructure needed, first, to bring school and community together in a strong, collaborative, and cohesive way, and then, to guide, support, monitor and study, and modify, as indicated, individual and social environment change efforts. A framework like an EES is needed that systematically generates knowledge and transmits best practice principles to designated groups but allows participants in particular places to modify practices, when justified, to meet particular local needs. This would give such programs a focused sense of purpose and direction and make them more efficient, effective, and cost-effective—and, thus, more sustainable. Without an EES-like framework that makes development possible in many ways and in many places simultaneously, in little boutiques of effort, such as our SDP, we will keep discovering what we already know, what my unlettered mother knew years ago—children perform well when caretakers provide them with a good experience.

The human service departments most involved in people development—social work, clinical psychology, nursing, and others—already exist in many schools of education or in their universities. As mentioned previously, the arts and sciences can strengthen the knowledge base of existing and pre-service educators and human service providers. Research programs at colleges and universities can give focused attention to more appropriate ways of understanding the effects of individual and institutional interactivity and feelings on social environment or context, and on individual and group behavior and performance. This will require public health, human ecology, and clinical perspectives and methods similar to what we used to bring about school culture or context changes in our School Development Program.

People development leads to the kind of social and political action needed to promote investment in personnel and appropriate training and to bring about a fair system of funding public education. Again, the needs of children performing well, desirous of a fair chance and backed by increasingly powerful forces, cannot be ignored indefinitely. Most Americans want to provide all children with a fair chance, but not by adding to their already strained budgets.

There is new and better curriculum, instruction, school management, and adult and student development knowledge available, but it is being resisted or being utilized in less than optimally effective ways primarily because we all but ignore child and adolescent development issues. This is largely because the professional identity of *teacher as instructor* rather than as *child and youth developer in the service of teaching and learning* is first established in schools of education and then reinforced in practice with colleagues who were similarly prepared. Thus, taking a developmental perspective is not something that comes naturally or easily in practice situations in which few hold it as a part of their identity.

This is the reason that it takes significant time and energy to promote and to sustain a focus on student development in schools. And it often goes away when the training, key supporters or other facilitating factors are removed. But if doing so were part of what it means to be a teacher or school leader, there would be little, if any, resistance. (Education agencies within schools of education would also be well positioned to help teachers and administrators already in practice incorporate new ways of working.) But the best chance to balance, perhaps fuse, the emphasis on curriculum, instruction, and assessment with that of child and youth development is during the initial professional development of educators—before they begin to teach or become school leaders.

Many view schools of education as a major source of inertia and resistance; I feel they are a major, well-connected, and strategically located resource. It was with this in mind that we looked to several schools of education to help us to disseminate our SDP model. When this approach proved successful, it occurred to me that this model could evolve into a mini-model of an Education Extension Service.

I envisioned a unit within schools of education serving as an extension service agency that could help primary and secondary schools and districts in its region apply child and youth development knowledge and skills to all aspects of their work—organization and management, the creation of a school culture that supports development, and the utilization of knowledge about development to structure and guide curricular activities and instruction. This would involve some of their senior faculty in real-world work or fieldwork. It would enable their students to work in schools under the supervision of faculty–district teacher collaborations. It would allow students and faculty to provide feedback that would, in turn, enable the university to modify their pre-service programs to better prepare future educators to work in the real world, to better support student development and learning.

Such an arrangement would also enable the arts and sciences, physical education, liberal arts, medicine, and other schools and departments within a university to work with local schools and districts in a planned and coordinated way. This approach, along with many other adjustments in how support services are provided to schools, could begin to address the problems of fragmentation, duplication, inefficiency, ineffectiveness, and waste involved in the underplanned, uncoordinated, poorly integrated way that services are now often provided.

It would also allow relationships to be established that would enable people and products and other resources from outside a particular school to be delivered in a more personal and emotionally meaningful way. For example, a growing number of business corporations and local businesses are providing summer internships in which students interact with employees and experience real world relationship and work, as well as gain a better appreciation of the connection between workplace demands and what they are learning in school. Without meaningful relationships, many talks and demonstrations in schools by outside people are not as useful as we think.

Our SDP program has had alliances with about ten schools of education. Units headed by senior staff from these schools have helped districts implement the SDP without our Yale team's presence on an ongoing basis. All the dissemination arrangements—youth service organizations, education departments, school district units—have had numerous successes, but because schools of education can prepare large numbers of future teachers and administrators, they have the highest potential for promoting large-scale change. On the other hand, the collaboration with Youth Guidance, which had impressive outcomes from using social workers, underscores the need to prepare professional support staff in such a way that they can help other professionals create school cultures that help staff and parents function well and help students grow.

Our experience with the partnerships between Eastern Michigan University (EMU) and Detroit; C. W. Post University and Westbury, New York; and Drury University and Springfield, Missouri, suggests that full-blown model educational extension agencies could be developed. In all three of these instances, child and adolescent development–focused changes have taken place in university-based pre-service curricula and teaching, in the in-service internships of students under senior faculty supervision, and in in-service support of their school district partners.

At Drury, in particular, other departments have served the school district through collaborations with the school of education. All our university partners have made some internal changes. A master's program based on the SDP was created at the University of Illinois, Chicago. A free master's program for teachers working in schools using the SDP was created at Drury. It attracted new teachers, improved retention, and improved teaching and achievement outcomes. This incentive suggests a way to promote a focus on child and youth development.

In addition to the agency component at the colleges that I have described, our EES mini-model included a provision for an interdisciplinary council at the Yale Child Study Center, a summer policy institute, and an instructional program that evolved from our original Social Skills Curriculum program and deepened our effort to integrate development and instruction (the Comer in the

Classroom approach). Our intent is to create a school curriculum that integrates developmental and academic teaching and learning from preschool to maturity, perhaps through college.

The purpose of the interdisciplinary council component is to expand the knowledge base of education by involving basic and clinical researchers with practitioners in mutually beneficial ways. Our colleagues at the Yale Child Study Center represent the mix we had in mind—geneticists, neurochemists, epidemiologists, and others. We are particularly interested in the implications of modern brain research for teaching and learning. Indeed, one of the reasons that education is often a second-class citizen in the academy, and a football in the political arena, is that it is not strongly rooted in its natural basic science—child development. I suspect that if this were the case, most of what I have discussed in this book would already be widespread education practice.

The absence of basic science anchoring and of arts and science connections contributes to the charge that educators are intellectually narrow, or worse. It is a bum rap. The tiny bit of research I have seen does not support this claim. But if there is a problem, I suspect that we will do more to broaden the interests and perspectives of educators by bringing these university-based disciplines into education than by sending future educators into classrooms to hear lectures devoid of real-world school context and knowledge application, courses that will be too superficial to provide the disciplinary components that make the knowledge useful in practice. This is more possible where a part of a school of education is serving as a component of an EES.

We realized early in our work that, like most educators, policy-makers, business and opinion leaders, and the general public know very little about child development, its relevance to school learning, or how to promote it. This has serious negative consequences for education. The intent of our EES-like summer institute was to create an opportunity for policymakers and practitioners to talk to each other, to promote mutual understanding and improved relationships. An experience I had at EMU suggests both interest and possibilities.

The chair of the Education Leadership Department arranged for me to address school board members in a small, rural county of Michigan. During the discussion, and as a response to my appeal for attention to child development, a board member stood, agreed with the need, and suggested to the chair that the university create a child development–related course for school board members. That is exactly what the agricultural agents did one hundred years ago to help overcome the inertia and resistance to improvements in farming.

We have held three summer institutes, one in New York City and two in Washington, D.C. The second included a session on Capitol Hill sponsored by Congresswoman Sheila Jackson Lee, then the chairperson of the Children's Caucus in the House of Representatives. In the two years, about twenty members of Congress have shared their perspectives with us. Participants have heard from representatives of parents; students; teacher and administrator unions; boards of education; businesses; foundations; and local, state, and federal policymakers.

Dr. Valerie Maholmes provided leadership for this work and is currently doing an assessment of the effectiveness during the 2003–04 academic year. The reflections on our EES-like work suggest that it can be an effective way to address the several critical obstacles blocking large-scale school improvement, and they support our notion that schools of education should provide the central ingredient—the education agency. Again, why schools of education? Willie Sutton robbed banks because "that's where the money is." Schools of education must play the key role in an EES approach because most of the nation's 3 million teachers and administrators, and many of the professional support people that make up the only reasonably reliable resource we have to continue the development of students, passed through them and will continue to do so. Also, they are connected to other child knowledge bases, with private and public oversight arrangements, in a way that other preparatory programs are not. These connections and conditions are particularly important at a time when biotechnological discoveries about the brain and mind, with implications for teaching and learning, are rapidly taking place.

Our EES mini-model is not grandiosity, I hope. Successful ideas hatched and incubated in mini-models have a chance of growing to the point that they inform large-scale change.

Most schools of education will need to make significant adjustments in order to be effective as education agencies—indeed, simply to be effective schools of education. Over the past fifteen years or so, there has been much good thinking among educators about how to improve curriculum, instruction, and assessment, including the use of technology in the service of these activities. I emphasize this point because too often technology is put forth, by educators and politicians alike, as the magic button or sign of enlightenment that will save education rather than as a facilitation tool, which it really is.

There has been much, much less thought about child and youth development beyond developmentally appropriate teaching. The thinking that has been done is usually limited to interactions between teacher and child, sometimes about interactions with other children and behaviors in the classroom. Very rarely does it extend to how every aspect of school functioning can be used to promote child and youth development. Instructional communities and communities that promote development and learning are not the same thing. The latter are more likely to help many more students to enjoy an experience in school that will enable them to meet their adult tasks and responsibilities.

Policymakers often talk about creating large-scale change programs based on successful project models. But even with a strong focus on promoting development, what works in one place with a particular group of people may not work in the next (Sizer, 1999).

An Education Extension Service approach, combined with school-based, community-based, and agency alliances and with political action, constitutes the kind of change strategy that could make a great positive difference by reducing the forces of resistance; creating a present and future education workforce capable of using proven approaches to connect with families and community-based organizations in a way that enables them to collectively support the development and learning of all students; and promoting fair and coherent education policy. This would give many more students an opportunity to experience the American dream, to have the stake in it needed to make it worth protecting, and to reduce the high cost of preventable problem behaviors. Although much of our SDP work has been in low-income and minority communities, some of it has been in middle-income communities; the difference in needs is only a matter of degree and time.

Great teams fail to win the play-off game when they abandon the strategies that got them there. Today, America is a better democracy and a superpower in large part because of policies and practices that enabled an ever-increasing number of people to benefit from the rule of law and reasonable access to the economic and educational conditions that made personal, family, and community well-being possible. Great civilizations can begin to decline when they stop doing what got them there. We can and must preserve desired conditions for most, and we must provide opportunity for the children and families left behind. We will leave no child behind when we close the gap between the support for development and learning that today's children need to perform well in today's and tomorrow's world and what they are actually receiving.

References

Dryfoos, J. G. *Full-Service Schools: A Revolution in Health and Social Services for Children, Youth, and Families.* San Francisco: Jossey-Bass, 1998.

Sizer, T. R. Horace's Hope: *What Works for the American High School.* New York: Houghton Mifflin, 1996.

Sizer, T. R. "No Two Are Quite Alike." *Educational Leadership,* September 1999, 57:1, 6–11.

Smith, A. "An Inquiry into the Nature and Causes of the Wealth and Nations." (E. Cannan, ed.) London: Methuen, 1904. Retrieved from http://www.econlib.org/library/Smith/smWN1.html.

7

All Our Children

The election of our first African American president twenty years after *Maggie's American Dream* was written is a testament to the progress America has made. And an education that prepares all children to meet the challenges and opportunities of adult life is now more important than ever before if we are to continue to move beyond black and white, and if our unique experiment in democracy and humanism is to survive and thrive into the distant future.

THREE YEARS AGO, I WAS INVITED TO THE MARTIN LUTHER KING Day ceremonies at our original project site, the Martin Luther King Jr. Elementary School. The thirty students in the gospel choir were dressed in white blouses, shirts, and dark pants. They were handsome children, their faces beaming, and they were singing with enthusiasm and excitement. One young lady, Martha, stood out. Among the numbers, they sang, "This land is your land; this land is my land." She sang the song with a special gusto, swaying back and forth with an intensity and a sincerity that reminded me of myself forty years before. She had a dream.

Her spirit and desire made me hopeful and apprehensive at the same time. Yes, this land is her land, but it isn't to the degree that it should be for black people. I admire my mother and father and the many black parents who climbed every mountain, forded every stream, who kept on keeping on in the face of race-related obstacles so that their children could have the opportunities available to every other American. But that is no way to run a country.

The unnecessary obstacles blacks faced—and continue to face—mean that America loses the skills and contributions of too many. That's what happened with my childhood friends—Nathan English, who died early from alcoholism; Madison Turner, who has been in and out of mental institutions all of his life; and Rudy George, who spent a good part of his life in jail for murder. A trickle make it when it should be a mighty flood.

At the same time, the conditions that made even the trickle possible are eroding. The steel mills that allowed my father to earn a reasonable living are all but silent now; the industrial base of the nation has shrunk. The three-generation movement from uneducated to highly educated that the industrial economy made possible is much more difficult for families and groups to undergo today. Schools, child care, housing, and social service programs have not been adjusted to make it possible for children and families to function at the level needed in this postindustrial age. What it took to make our two schools work is striking evidence of this problem.

Life in a world changing ever faster because of science and technology is like a relay race with each generation almost desperately passing the baton on to the next. Past and present policies and practices which made it extremely difficult for black Americans to achieve at the level of their ability are like dropping the baton. And black America is not another team in competition with America. Black Americans are a part of America's team. If America keeps running without the baton, no matter how fast or how far, we're going to lose. Black young people with skills and abilities are all our children. And until they can sing, "This land is my land; this land is your land" and that's a fact, we, America, will not thrive at the level of our potential. Many things must be done to realize our potential. Helping our schools prepare all our children to thrive as adults is one of the most important.

QUESTIONS FOR REFLECTION

1. Why has school integration on its own not been enough to create a level playing field for all students?
2. Dr. Comer asserts that a certain level of nurturance is necessary to enable children to succeed in education and in life. Given that many students' homes and communities do not provide the necessary socialization, how can schools, teachers, and community service organizations help fulfill that need?
3. Why is an understanding of child development essential for educators, especially for those working with children who lack family and social networks that prepare them for formal education?
4. Why is a school's culture important in determining whether its students succeed or fail at learning?
5. The story of the young man in "Me, Walter, and America" (Chapter Two) goes back forty years. Would Walter's story be different if he were a young man today? If so, how?
6. Dr. Comer and his colleagues began developing their School Development Program (SDP) framework more than

157

forty years ago. Given the program's positive outcomes in hundreds of schools, what has kept its principles from being adopted more widely?

7. Why are measurements of academic achievement alone insufficient to judge whether a school intervention program is working?

8. Dr. Comer states that a strong planning and management team made up of teachers, parents, administrators, and other school staff is essential to a successful implementation of SDP. Why is this so? What does such a collaborative structure accomplish?

9. Why must the shift to a child development focus begin with the learning that teachers receive in schools of education?

10. If Dr. Comer's ideas were put into widespread practice next year, how long do you think it would be before we would see results? What would those results be? What would the United States look like in ten years? Twenty years?

Index

THE AUTHOR

James P. Comer is the Maurice Falk Professor of Child Psychiatry at the Yale University School of Medicine's Child Study Center. He has concentrated his career on promoting a focus on child development as a way of improving schools. He is perhaps best known for founding the Comer School Development Program, which promotes the collaboration of parents, educators, and community to improve social, emotional, and academic outcomes for children that, in turn, helps them achieve greater school success. Dr. Comer has authored nine books and has written more than 150 articles for *Parents Magazine* and more than 300 syndicated articles on children's health and development and race relations. For his work and scholarship, Dr. Comer has been awarded forty-seven honorary degrees and has been recognized by many organizations. In 2007 he received the Grawemeyer Award for Education. He's also received the John P. McGovern Behavioral Science Award from the Smithsonian and the John Hope Franklin Award, given to those who have demonstrated the highest commitment to access and excellence in American education.

TITLES IN THE JOSSEY-BASS
OUTSTANDING IDEAS IN EDUCATION
SERIES

Literacy and Learning
Reflections on Writing, Reading, and Society

By Deborah Brandt

Deborah Brandt is one of the most influential figures in literacy and education. Brandt has dedicated her career to the status of reading and writing in the United States. Her literacy research is renowned and widely studied. *Literacy and Learning* is an important collection of Brandt's work that includes a combination of previously published essays, previously unpublished talks, and new work.

All the selected essays focus on changes in perspectives and perceptions about reading and writing. Throughout the book, Brandt describes how literacy skills have become intertwined with economic competition and technological change, how basic skills in one generation often prove inadequate for the next—and the tremendous pressure this puts on teachers, families, communities and, most of all, learners. In addition, Brandt introduces the concept of sponsors of literacy—agents, forces, and institutions that stimulate or support people's literacy strivings for their own economic or political or cultural advantage.

Literacy and Learning is a compelling and thought-provoking reflection on the changing definitions and expectations for literacy in recent years. It elevates key debates in education to include a broader social awareness.

ISBN: 978-0-470-40134-7 • Hardcover